A ◆ B G C ◆ M O N O G R A P H

Partners in the Gospel

◆

THE STRATEGIC ROLE
OF PARTNERSHIP
IN WORLD
EVANGELIZATION

EDITED BY

JAMES H. KRAAKEVIK & DOTSEY WELLIVER

Partners in the Gospel

The Strategic Role of Partnership in World Evangelization

© by the Billy Graham Center, Wheaton College
Printed in the United States of America

ISBN 1–879089–11–4

Contents

Contributors

Panya Baba is President of the Evangelical Church of West Africa with more than 2,000,000 members in some 3,000 churches across Nigeria. Rev. Baba has served as a pastor and evangelist, receiving training in Nigerian Bible schools and in All Nations Bible College in England. He is an international missions leaders, having spoken at Lausanne '89 in Manila and is active in the "World by 2000" movement.

Luis Bush is International Director of the A.D. 2000 and Beyond Movement. His deep desire is to see the church of Jesus Christ planted among every unreached people group. He is a leading evangelical thinker and has written numerous articles and books including *Partnering in Ministry* and *Funding Third-World Missions*.

Phill Butler is founder and Executive Director of InterDev in Seattle, Washington—an organization which works to coordinate missions efforts, particularly in the Two-Thirds world. He has had broad experience in communications, having worked as an international news correspondent and manager of commercial radio stations. He is known for his many years of overseas experience and excellent managerial skills.

Met Castillo holds a Doctor of Missiology degree and is a frequent speaker at international missions conferences. He is general secretary for the Philippine Missions Association and also serves with the Philippine Evangelical Fellowship.

Keith Fraser-Smith is an ordained Church of England evangelical minister who has worked for 16 years in the region of the world from which he draws his case study. He was a founding member of the Strategic Evangelism Partnership which he describes in his paper and has been the facilitator of several of its working groups.

David Garrison is Director of the Nonresidential Missionary Program of Cooperative Services International for the Southern Baptist Church. He formerly taught at a Baptist college in Hong Kong. He has an M.Div. from Golden Gate Baptist Theological Seminary and holds a Ph.D. in historical theology from the University of Chicago.

James Glynn is pastor of the Cross & Crown Community Church in Arlington Heights, Illinois. He has a B.A. from Wittenberg University and an M.Div. from Luther-Northwestern Theological Seminary. He is active in motivating his congregation to become involved in Missions.

Ian M. Hay is General Director of SIM International. He earned his Doctor of Missiology degree from Trinity Evangelical Divinity School. He is a frequent speaker at missions conferences and consultations.

W. Valjene Hayworth, on the pastoral staff at the Elmbrook Church in Waukesha, Wisconsin, coordinates the missions ministry. Leaving his role as a musician with the Milwaukee Symphony, Val, his wife Suzanne, and their three children served for seven years in Iran as self-supporting missionaries.

Larry Keyes holds a Doctor of Missiology degree from Fuller Theological Seminary School of World Mission. While Field Leader for OC Ministries in Brazil, he developed a national ministry of leadership training in church growth. He is presently president of OC Ministries.

Myung H. Kim is General Secretary of Korea Evangelical Fellowship and Associate General Secretary of the Korean World Missions Association. He holds master's degrees in church history from Westminster Theological Seminary and Yale Divinity School and earned his Ph.D. in Patristics from the Aquinas Institute of Theology.

James H. Kraakevik, former director of Research and Ministries for SIM International, has been director of the Billy Graham Center at Wheaton College since 1984. He earned his Ph.D. in Physics from the University of Maryland, taught at Wheaton College, and with his wife Lynn and five sons, served in Nigeria from 1964 - 1970.

John Kyle is Coordinator for the Presbyterian Church in America Mission to the World. As former Director of InterVarsity Missions, he challenged students to become involved in completing the task of reaching the lost for Jesus Christ. He has authored several books, including *Urban Mission: God's Concern for the City* (Downers Grove, IL: InterVarsity Press, 1988).

David Mays is Great Lakes Regional Director for Advancing Churches and Missions Commitment (ACMC—formerly Association of Church Missions Committees). He works with churches in five states—speaking, consulting, and organizing training conferences to advance missions in the local church.

James Moats is President of Issachar and has a deep interest in reaching unreached peoples groups. Issachar assists local churches in developing a focus on unreached people.

George Otis, Jr., is President of the Sentinel Group in Lynnwood, Washington. His latest book is *The Last of the Giants* (Chosen Books, 1991).

Dr. Larry Pate is the President of the Peoples Mission International and a recognized authority in the area of missions from the Two-Thirds World. He has authored four books and numerous articles. His *From Every People* (MARC, 1989) was selected by *World Christian* magazine as one of the five best books on missions for 1989. He is also editor of *Bridging Peoples*, an international newsletter for the leaders of non-Western missions.

Dotsey Welliver is Editorial Coordinator at the Billy Graham Center at Wheaton College, Wheaton, IL. She has a B.A. in psychology from Azusa Pacific University and holds the M.A. in communications from Wheaton Graduate School. She has authored seven family-oriented inspirational books and numerous devotional articles.

Acknowledgments

We would like to express our appreciation to Brad Smith who did excellent editorial work on earlier portions of this manuscript.

Our thanks go also to *Pulse* for permission to reprint the article contained in Appendix C. And a special word of gratitude goes to Keith Fraser-Smith, InterDev, Issachar, and Larry Pate for the use of their charts and illustrations.

Foreword

I never thought it would happen. For all of its fifteen-year existence, Apple Computer Inc. pursued its own personal computer technology and was IBM's primary competitor in that market. Apple was as different in the public image to IBM as Frank Sinatra was to the Grateful Dead. IBM has been the button-down standard for corporate America while Apple, with its rainbow-colored logo, has sold itself as the innovative maker of "insanely great" computers for "the rest of us." Throughout their competitive existence, the two worked on different systems and sold different software packages preventing one program from operating on the other system in order to gain market share.

But on July 3, 1991, the surprise announcement was made. Apple and IBM entered into a partnership agreement which will virtually rewrite the computer industry's rules. For years, Apple and IBM watched as personality clashes, shifting technologies, and the success of local upstarts threatened their hold on the very market they had invented. With slipping market share in a slow economy, the two companies began their long march together to reclaim that market.

This new partnership will not be easy. So many issues demand agreement. Yet both companies stand to win big worldwide while each company maintains its own identity and specialty. This is a timely and significant partnership. Together they will be more effective than were they to remain separate and mutually competitive.

This new partnership is important as an illustration of what is happening, not only in business, but also in missions today. Around the world, mission agencies which have been involved in individual pursuits and have promoted their own agendas are now sensing unusual pressures from limited resources and the missionary success of local or global religions.

Several areas in the world where Christianity has been tradition-ally strong have succumbed to the secularistic spirit of our age and adversely influenced those in the next generation. In order to see new spiritual advances with the gospel, or even to maintain organizational survival in our harsh world, the collective philosophy of missionary partnership has become a stronger impulse in ministry. The time has come for mission groups to work together on projects and tasks while maintaining their own separate identity.

In one sense, this is nothing new. For years, missionaries have talked about cooperation and partnership. But the "newness" in this dialogue today is found in the high motivation among Christian workers to take the dialogue from conference tables and convention halls and apply it in new ways with jointly accountable strategies on the mission field.

As one of the 159 participants stated before attending the National Missions Consultation in Singapore (May 2–4, 1991), "Is this going to be another talk-and-no-action project, or one that loses steam after one or two years?"[1] So far, the response has been "no." As Michael Jaffarian, executive director of the Singapore Center for Evangelism and Missions (SCEM) and a member of the consultation organizing committee stated, "What counts most is not what happened in those three days, but what happens over the coming years in missions and evangelization. We have many reasons for optimism—among them the new enthusiasm and spirit of cooperation that has emerged."[2]

From Discussion to Implementation

This, then, is what is new in the dialogue—a widespread desire to go beyond discussion to focus upon implementation. This desire appears to be clearly stated by both missionaries on the field and in conference documents.

This focus of going beyond mere discussion, for example, is envisioned for the 1992 SCUPE Congress in Chicago. Ever since the first Congress in 1978, the Seminary Consortium for Urban Pastoral Education (SCUPE) has provided a resource event for urban practitioners attracting 800–1,000 leaders from 50 denominations and more than 30 countries.

In 1992, the theme of the Congress is "Partnership." According to David Frenchak, Executive Director of SCUPE, the focus of this Congress will be upon offering "extensive insights and practical applications for forming partnerships...."[3] He writes, the Congress will "provide many opportunities to form new networks among urban practitioners."[4] The purpose is not merely to discuss but to forge new networks and partnership agreements in ministry in order to become more effective in our rapidly changing world.

The same was true concerning the conference sponsored by the World Evangelical Fellowship (WEF) Missions Commission in June, 1992. Top mission leaders of the Western and non-Western world gathered together under the theme "Toward Interdependent Partnership." The conference stressed the development of new partnership agreements by emphasizing mutual trust and understanding, bridges of relationships, networks for action, and specific partnership relationships.

No longer will it suffice for a conference on missionary cooperation to only discuss partnership. With limited resources and increased opposition, like IBM and Apple, the time has come when conferences must provide practical measures whereby specific cooperative projects or task-oriented partnerships are suggested and, hopefully, formed.

Working Consultation on Partnership at Wheaton, IL

It was into this growing evangelical mood for practical cooperative measures that James H. Kraakevik, Director of the Billy Graham Center (BGC), Wheaton College, Wheaton, Ill., and Phill Butler of InterDev, Seattle, suggested a special working consultation on partnership. Held May 9–11, 1991, it was to be a forum for sharing case studies of partnerships, both success stories and failures.

Sponsored by the Billy Graham Center in cooperation with the Interdenominational Foreign Mission Association (IFMA), the Evangelical Fellowship of Missions Agencies (EFMA), InterDev, and the Association of Church Missions Committees (ACMC), this Working Consultation focused on four areas:

- Strategic partnership in unreached areas of the world
- Partnership between churches in North America and churches overseas, with mission agencies often as bridges, for evangelism and church planting
- Partnership among traditional mission agencies and newer mission agencies from the developing churches of the Two-Thirds world
- Partnership among Two-Thirds world mission agencies.

It was anticipated that the consultation would produce working papers that would highlight principles and set guidelines for effective cooperation in evangelization within the unreached areas of the world.[5] The publication of this volume achieves that aim.

In order to accomplish these goals, the sixty-five participants from thirty-eight different organizations and eleven countries discussed four case studies of missionary partnership — each one focusing upon one of the consultation's four areas of study. After presenting each study, the participants were able to apply and implement the lessons learned in smaller workshops.

Phill Butler of InterDev, for example, worked with a group on the first subject: integrated partnerships. After the workshop, he reported that seven partnerships between more than 100 agencies are in place, with "another five or six forming and 10 to 12 pending."[6]

Val Hayworth of Elmbrook Church, Waukesha, Wisconsin indicated that church-to-church partnerships are just getting started. He said that "his church is trying to partner with a church in Soviet Central Asia. The church sent people to the Moscow Congress on Soviet Evangelization last October and identified a potential sister church in Frunze, Kirghizia. The goal is a joint evangelistic outreach in the area."[7]

Ian Hay of SIM International worked on the third subject: partnership among traditional mission agencies and newer mission agencies from the developing churches of the Two-Thirds world. He indicated that "his agency partners with the Evangelical Church of West Africa (ECWA has 2,200 churches, 900 missionaries), with four German mission societies, and with two denominations in Korea that have sent 31 missionaries to SIM."[8]

Hay stated that "the major part of world missions has to be related to the church around the world. The total church must be mobilized. The wave of the future is, How do we work together?"[9]

Throughout the consultation practical illustrations of partnership agreements were shared on all four of the selected themes. By the end of the three days of reflection, a collective statement was written which affirmed:

"We commit ourselves to explore and develop new partnerships for world evangelization, so that

...all remaining unreached and least evangelized peoples will be reached;

...missions-active churches will be planted among those peoples; all churches, agencies, movements, institutions, and structures will be better mobilized toward the fulfillment of the Great Commission."[10]

Note that this theme emphasizes their commitment to implement new missionary partnerships. This statement fits into the growing "mood of the times" where missionaries desire less discussion and more application of missionary cooperation. This theme runs throughout the Consultation papers in this book.

Implications for Ministry

In Africa, I am told, they have a proverb which states that "no situation is permanent." Change is part of everyday life. So it is with us in world missions. The increased involvement in interagency cooperation both at home and abroad is the trend today. As Paul Hiebert of Trinity Evangelical Divinity School once said, "The future of missions is based in the formation of international networks rather than multinational organizations. Networks build up people, not programmes; they stress partnership and servanthood, not hierarchy; they help to build up the local church, not undermine it."[11]

These papers from the Working Consultation on Partnership suggest different ways networks can be applied to missionary activity. One way is to establish cooperative agreements among groups which belong, historically, to the same missionary tradition or theological perspective. SIM International (SIM), for example, has many cooperative agreements with the Evangelical Church of West Africa (ECWA)— an autonomous church body which was born out of the ministry of SIM. Several illustrations of this type are found in this literature.

A second kind of network or cooperative partnership suggested is among members of one loosely structured association. An example is the Association of Evangelicals of Africa and Madagascar (AEAM). Many diverse denominations and agencies cooperate together in evangelistic and social concerns because of a common identity and general philosophy of ministry. This has allowed AEAM to send teams of workers representing many different agencies and nationalities to at least twelve countries to help churches in women's ministries, management, pastoral roles, evangelistic efforts, and youth work.

A third kind of missionary network, and perhaps the most popular mentioned at the Wheaton Consultation, is the task-based partnership. This venture is based, not only on historical affiliation, membership in an association, or even geographical proximity to need, but also on a common commitment to the accomplishment of specific tasks. The unreached people movement, for example, represents a worldwide commitment to a common focus and many groups are cooperating together whether on local, regional, or international levels.

It was this type of partnership focus which encouraged the mission organization, Calvary Ministries, to work with WEC International in a joint survey trip to discern the mind of the Lord in evangelizing together the country of Guinea-Bissau. And this kind of partnership encouraged the development of a working agreement in India between the Baptist Christian Association, the Zoram Baptist Mission, and the Conservative Baptist Foreign Mission Society. These three agencies, along with the Church Growth Missionary Society, planned a joint task of evangelizing the Korku tribal people in Central India.

As you read the papers in this book and reflect upon the various kinds of network partnerships, it will become evident that many of the cooperative structures are formed to assist in research and evangelistic activity. It seems that missionaries have become very willing to share information and cooperate in reaching the yet unreached peoples, irrespective of denominational affiliation or agency identity.

As Tokunboh Adeyemo, General Secretary of AEAM, recently stated, "I don't care who gets the recognition, as long as the Gospel is preached and God is glorified."[12]

There are other important areas for networking and interagency cooperation not referred to often in this volume. What about the topic of missionary training, for example? This cooperative venture could either be short- or long-term, through seminars or degree granting programs. It could work through residency or extension centers, involve teaching in person or by tape, through translator or in translated publications. The variations are many. But if we experience the expected rise in missionary complexity as we enter the twenty-first century, partnership in missionary training between Western and non-Western workers will be critical.

Or how about the difficult area of cooperative funding? Suspicion and the fear of being controlled or used often exist when entering an agreement of mutual funding for a project. Financial trust must be built and procedures made more flexible, particularly if those involved represent diverse cultures.

With governmental restrictions hindering the transfer of money from certain countries, with limited financial resources handicapping quick response to special field need, with inflation placing additional pressure upon the cost of evangelistic projects, and with the expense of training missionary candidates increasing, the time has come to assess our willingness to consider international financial partnerships. The Wheaton Consultation has helped to begin this process. Much more can be done.

What about our willingness to cooperate in our mission publicity? How about publicly stating the accomplishments and successes of other groups in our own missionary publications by giving due acknowledgment of the role other groups had in "our" ministry success?

Writer and missionary educator Michael Griffiths states, "So often we only know what our own group is doing. I remember being asked at a college in Canada whether I know the missionaries in Japan. I asked who they meant and they named three couples whom I happened to have met. I replied that I knew several hundred of the 2,500 missionaries working in that country, but they behaved as though their own six from their denomination were all there were."[13]

In applying his comment, Griffiths continued, "I know of only a few missionary magazines which regularly make a point of mentioning sister societies working in the same area, even when they actually cooperate on the field. This is part of the problem of a success-oriented public relations, which puffs up successes and makes big news items of them with singular lack of objectivity about actual achievement."[14]

This Working Consultation on Partnership at BGC contributed important information and motivated many toward more effective interagency cooperation. In Scripture, our Lord shared with His disciples, "... I pray also for those who will believe in me through (the disciples) message, that all of them may be one, Father, just as you are in me and I am in you" (John 17:20–21). The Consultation helped to demonstrate in tangible ways this spiritual unity which we all enjoy with believers around the world.

The sessions evidenced that the world of missions is becoming more interdependent. Traditional differences between West and non-West are fading as new issues of mission compatibility or non-compatibility surface. Cross-cultural workers are placing more value upon networks and partnerships and less upon organizational structures and hierarchies. Conferences are being assessed by their practicality and usefulness while ministry resources are no longer limited to one's own group.

We trust this book becomes an encouragement and a resource to you as you work with others toward accomplishing the Great Commission. We hope its information will help, not to impose our partnership agendas upon leaders with whom we wish to partner, but rather to guide us toward developing stronger relationships with those among whom we desire to work. And our prayer is that, with the insights gained from this Consultation, we will be more effective in our evangelistic and church planting tasks, for God's glory and for the growth of His church.

Larry E. Keyes

Endnotes

[1] Stan Guthrie, "Singapore Talk Lays Groundwork for Action," in *Pulse*, Vol. 26, No. 12, (Wheaton, Ill.: Evangelical Missions Information Service, June 28, 1991), 2.

[2] Ibid.

[3] Cited from a letter by Dr. David J. Frenchak, Executive Director of SCUPE, dated 28 May, 1991, 1.

[4] Ibid.

[5] The above paragraph is taken from the basic document for the consultation entitled "Partnership for World Evangelization: A working Consultation," May, 1991, 1.

[6] James Reapsome, "Partnerships are crucial to success of missions, consultation declares," *Pulse*, Vol. 26, No. 11, (Wheaton, Ill.: Evangelical Missions Information Service, June 14, 1991), 5.

[7] Ibid.

[8] Ibid.

[9] Ibid.

[10] From "Partnership for World Evangelization: A Working Consultation," Summary Document from the Consultation at the Billy Graham Center, May 11, 1991, 2.

[11] Paul Hiebert, quoted in the *Haggai News*, March-April, (Singapore: Haggai Institute, 1983).

[12] Tokunboh Adeyemo, quoted in *Afroscope*, No. 40, April-June (Nairobi, Kenya: Association of Evangelicals of Africa and Madagascar, 1987), 1.

[13] "Michael Griffiths, "Inaugural Address: Hindrances To The Gospel," in *Seeds of Promise*, Allan Starling, Editor, (Pasadena, Calif.: William Carey Library, 1981), 42.

[14] Ibid.

Preface

In conversations between Phill Butler of InterDev and myself during 1990, discussion indicated the potential usefulness of a working consultation on partnership in world evangelization. Then a number of mission executives met together at the joint Evangelical Foreign Missions Association (EFMA)/Interdenominational Foreign Mission Association (IFMA) triennial meeting in September 1990 to discuss the need and to affirm their support. Therefore, a proposal was made to hold such a consultation at the Billy Graham Center at Wheaton College, Wheaton, Illinois, USA, May 9-11, 1991.

A steering committee was formed, consisting of Paul McKaughan (EFMA), Jack Frizen (IFMA), Bill Waldrop (ACMC), Luis Bush (Partners International), Larry Keyes (OC Ministries, Inc.), Phill Butler and Rick Stoller (Interdev), and Jim Kraakevik (Billy Graham Center).

The purpose was to hold a working consultation to address the following areas: 1) integrated partnerships to evangelize less reached peoples of the world, involving mission and national church agencies; 2) partnerships between North American churches and their counterparts overseas, with mission agencies often serving as bridges, for evangelism and church plantings; 3) partnerships among traditional Western mission agencies and newer missions from the developing churches of the Two-Thirds world; and 4) partnerships among Two-Thirds world mission agencies. The consultation had four short-term objectives:

1. To increase the awareness of opportunities, issues, benefits, and current status of the partnership approach to evangelism, focusing particularly on application to lesser reached ethnic groups;
2. To increase the number of ministries and institutions willing to explore involvement in partnerships;

3. To involve mission agencies in identifying and developing church-to-church and mission-to-mission relationships to facilitate cooperation in area-specific evangelism;

4. To identify specific steps that will encourage language specific partnerships in each region of critical concern.

The long-term objectives were:

1. To increase the number of unreached language groups where an effective, long-term, comprehensive witness is established.

2. As a result of God's work through effective partnerships, to see a nationally-led, reproducing church in each language group.

These were ambitious objectives. Some of the objectives were realized. Time will tell whether others will be accomplished. But this book is an attempt to share our vision with a wider public.

The Consultation was held as scheduled with more than 60 participants representing 48 agencies and 8 North American churches, from 12 countries and five continents. The program included:

- presentations of existing, functional, long-term partnership experiences among Christian agencies
- lessons to be learned from these experiences
- guidelines which could be produced to assist agencies in developing partnership relationships
- some action steps necessary to substantially increase the partnership approach to church-planting strategies

The format consisted of an introduction of Biblical foundations, followed by a presentation of basic principles and case studies in each of the four areas of Integrated Partnerships, Church-to-Church Partnerships, Mission-to-Mission Partnerships, and Two-Thirds World Partnerships. In each area working groups were formed to deal with issues related to that area. The presentations, case studies, and working group reports form the basis of this book.

The consultation concluded with a time of prayer for God's Spirit to empower and enable us to work together. The participants then approved a statement of acknowledgment, confession, and affirmation (see Appendix A).

As an introduction to the Consultation, key trends facing the world and the church were presented. Gordon Aeschliman has listed some in *Global Trends* (InterVarsity Press, 1990): a shrinking world, the

Islamic revolution, democracy movements, the urban challenge, the dismantled Soviet empire, the fading glory of the West, and the internationalization of the Gospel. George Barna, in *Seven Trends Facing the Church in 1990 and Beyond* (*National and International Religion Report*, Stephen M. Wike, Publisher) presents other factors: emphasis on the family, quest for lasting relationships, decline of media ministries, shrinking of the support base, polarization—evangelical and ecumenical, and government involvement in church affairs.

We noted God's example of diversity through his creation, as presented in Psalm 8:3 and 19:1. The work of the lowly ant in planning and cooperation in Proverbs 6:6-8 is an example of synergy, where the result is greater than the sum of its parts. The principle of partnership is expressed in I Corinthians 3:9, "We are God's fellow workers." Thus we are in partnership with God *and* with one another. God is not interested in uniformity or homogeneity. He is too creative for that. He does, however, exhort us to unity. We must give up our obsession for independence and become more interdependent.

We trust that the following chapters will challenge you to think and take appropriate action that will increase kingdom synergy through partnering to bring glory to God and be a witness to the world.

James H. Kraakevik

Abbreviations

ACMC	Advancing Churches and Missions Commitment (formerly Association of Church Missions Committees)
AEAM	Association of Evangelicals of Africa and Madagascar
AMA	Asian Mission Association
AMC	Asian Missions Congress
BGC	Billy Graham Center, Wheaton College, Wheaton, Illinois
C&MA	Christian and Missionary Alliance
CCT	Church of Christ, Thailand
DMG	Deutsche Missions Gemeinschaft
ECWA	Evangelical Churches of West Africa
EFA	Evangelical Fellowship of Asia
EFMA	Evangelical Fellowship of Mission Agencies (formerly Evangelical Foreign Missions Association)
EFT	Evangelical Fellowship of Thailand
EMS	Evangelical Missionary Society, Nigeria
FMC	Faith Missions Church
IAM	International Afghan Mission
IFMA	Interdenominational Foreign Mission Association
IMF	Indonesian Missionary Fellowship
JEA	Japan Evangelical Association
JOMA	Japan Overseas Missions Association
KIM	Korea International Mission
KPMF	Korea Partnership Missions Fellowship
KWMA	Korean World Missions Association
NECF	National Evangelical Christian Fellowship, Malaysia
NEMA	Nigeria Evangelical Missions Association
NEMI	Nigeria Evangelical Missionary Institute
OM	Operation Mobilization
OMF	Overseas Missionary Fellowship
PMA	Philippine Missions Association
SCEM	Singapore Center for Evangelism and Missions
SCUPE	Seminary Consortium for Urban Pastoral Education
SEP	Strategic Evangelism Partnership
TEAM	The Evangelical Alliance Mission
UMCA	United Missionary Church Association
WEF	World Evangelical Fellowship

Section 1

❖❖❖

Introduction

CHAPTER 1

In Pursuit of True Christian Partnership: A Biblical Basis from Philippians

Luis Bush

Abstract: *Biblical partnership is defined as an association of two or more Christian autonomous bodies who have formed a trusting relationship and fulfill agreed-upon expectations by sharing complementary strengths and resources to reach their mutual goal. The theme of Philippians is joy in Christian partnership.*

Partnership Not An Option

Partnership is no longer an option. The Scriptures underscore the value of Christian partnership in advancing the gospel around the world. A changing world requires it. The Christian community increasingly demands it.

As historians reflect back, one of the watershed Christian documents of this century will likely be the *Lausanne Covenant*, produced in 1974 at the Lausanne I Conference. Following the event, *Time* magazine called it "a formidable forum, probably the widest ranging meeting ever held."

In a booklet on the Lausanne Movement prepared for the Lausanne II Conference held in 1989 in Manila, the writers suggested that perhaps the single most important outcome of the Congress was the *Lausanne Covenant*. Embedded within the fourteen affirmations one of the articles sticks out like a precious jewel because it is the only article that speaks of rejoicing. And just as in the book of Philippians, the reason for rejoicing is Christian partnership. Article eight, entitled "Churches in Evangelistic Partnership," reads as follows:

> We rejoice that a new missionary era has dawned. The dominant role of Western missions is fast disappearing. God is raising up from the younger churches a great new resource

for world evangelization and is thus demonstrating that the responsibility to evangelize belongs to the whole body of Christ.[1]

Since 1974, the dawn of partnership has become at least midmorning. This was noted recently by Wade Coggins, Executive Director of Evangelical Foreign Missions Association for thirty fruitful years, when he wrote a paper entitled "Accountability: Key to Partnership." He begins his paper with the words, "The desire for new and exciting partnerships in the nineties is loudly proclaimed and widely accepted. Indeed, it is likely *the most important single issue requiring creative thinking and action* in the decade ahead."

The biblical basis of true Christian partnership is contained in the Apostle Paul's letter to the church in Philippi. The Paul/Philippians partnership reveals the ingredients of successful partnerships for the twenty-first century. These are qualities that should be part of our partnerships, whether they be between individuals, churches, or missions.

In the almost two millennia since Paul wrote that letter, hundreds of commentators, students, and preachers have reflected upon the joy which is a major stream of thought running throughout this short letter. However, another recurring thought that threads its way through from the beginning to the end has rarely been observed and yet provides the undergirding reason for the joy. This theme is genuine Christian partnership.

The interweaving of the two major repeating thoughts of joy and partnership in Paul's inspired letter to the Philippians is underscored by the author from the outset. In the first chapter, immediately following the greeting, the writer expresses his joy (1:3–4). Over and over he refers to his joy (1:25, 2:2, 2:17, 2:18 [twice], 2:29, 3:1, 4:1, 4:4 [twice], and 4:10).

Why was Paul so joyful? One of the main reasons, if not the primary reason, was because of his partnership with the Christians in Philippi. Paul makes that clear not only at the outset as he introduces the letter (1:4–5) but also at the end as he concludes the letter (4:10). Paul's joy in partnership is spelled out in no uncertain terms in 4:1 when he writes "you are my joy and crown," referring to his partner in ministry.

The preposition, "therefore," introduces the concluding chapter and section of the thought the apostle is communicating, as if to say:

"After all that I have written to you, the bottom line is this...You yourselves, my partners in ministry, are the source of my joy and my reward."

This book is the most personal, familiar, and brotherly of all the general epistles of Paul. It is not so much a letter of an apostle to his flock as it is a brotherly letter to his family—a coworker writing to those with whom he has labored. It is a book about partnership in ministry at the deepest level. Paul had those he was partnering with in his heart (1:7).

Theme of Philippians is Joy in Christian Partnership

The theme is made plain to us in verse 5 of chapter 1, where Paul speaks of "the joy of your participation or partnership from the first day until now." Someone has captured the spirit of this theme calling it "the joy of joining in."

The grammatical structure of the first section of the letter indicates that "joy in partnership" is the controlling thought in the mind of the author. And after reading the entire epistle, one becomes conscious of the fact that the first section of introductory material is, in addition, a microcosm of the entire letter. Consequently, the controlling idea of the whole letter, as in the introductory section, is the "joy of genuine Christian partnership."

The content of the letter uncovers the essential ingredients of the partnership that made Paul rejoice again and again and will make those involved in similar partnerships rejoice greatly. In fact Philippians could be called "a manual on genuine Christian partnership."

Essential Ingredients of Genuine Christian Partnership

The essential ingredients of a genuine Christian partnership are presented in a progression of thought in the book of Philippians:

1) The meaning of Christian partnership (1:1–11)
2) The goal of Christian partnership (1:12, 1:5)
3) The foundation (1:12–24, 3:21)
4) The philosophy (1:2–1:11)
5) The tangibles in the development of Christian partnerships (2:12–19, 1:9–10, 4:10–17)
6) The intangibles in the development of Christian partnerships (2:19–4:7).

The meaning of Christian partnership — an association of two or more autonomous bodies (1:1–11)

Paul's introductory statement is foundational. He is saying: "We are partners together." We are partners first because we have been claimed together. We are saints; a people consecrated to God; God's covenant people (1:1–2). Secondly, we are partners because we have been called to serve the living God (1:1). And thirdly, we are partners because we have a common heritage.

Lydia hailed from the middle/upper class. A young woman manipulated by her owners was a slave from the lower class. And there was a jailer from the middle class. These three classes became one at the foot of the cross, where the ground is level.

Lydia was an Asiatic; the slave girl, a Greek; and the jailer, a Roman. The great truth of Christianity is powerfully illustrated here. In Christ there is neither "Jew nor Greek, neither bond nor free, neither male nor female." Regardless of race, nationality, gender, or socioeconomic level in society, we all share a common heritage. We are one at the foot of the cross. If we are to succeed in building the church through effective partnerships, we must celebrate this oneness.

And as we celebrate our oneness in Christ, we recognize that we are partners in the confirmation of the gospel (1:7). We struggle to keep out the anti-kingdom traits of power, parochialism, prestige, and possessions, as suggested by Dr. Sam Kamaleson who chairs the least-evangelized cities track of Countdown 2000. All of these traits are combated by the apostle Paul in this letter.

Tracing the root meaning of partnership. The Greek word (koinonia) used for partnership in Philippians can also be translated as "fellowship." Koinonia is derived from the word "koinonos" which means a "sharer." Koinonos in turn, is derived from the word "koinos" which means "common." A koinonia is an association of those who share something in common.

In Greek secular usage the word referred to marriage contracts and business relationships — agreements that involved sharing of privileges and responsibilities.

In the New Testament the word occurs twenty times and is found more frequently in the book of Philippians than in any other book. Normally, it is translated by the word "fellowship." Lightfoot comments that this is far more than a friendly atmosphere in a public meeting. The emphasis is joint-participation in an intimate relationship in which there is a common purpose. The word speaks of an association of two or more autonomous bodies.

Paul and the Philippian Christians had been working together in partnership for possibly ten to twelve years. They had gone to great efforts to communicate with each other, even sending emissaries back and forth over long treacherous miles, and the church out of its poverty had sent gifts for Paul's ministry. They had been constantly in each other's prayers as both worked to advance the gospel. The partnership was a deep source of joy to both — a sacred fellowship — bound together in common love for Christ and an urgency to make Him known.

A Definition of Partnership. A suggested biblical definition of Christian partnership might be "an association of two or more Christian autonomous bodies who have formed a trusting relationship and fulfill agreed-upon expectations by sharing complementary strengths and resources to reach their mutual goal."

The goal of Christian partnership — the advance of the Gospel (1:12, 1:5).

A unique partnership had been formed between Paul, the missionary, and the believers who fellowshipped together in Philippi. But Paul rejoiced in partnership not merely because he loved them and enjoyed their care and concern for him personally. He expressed his joy because they had partnered together in the Gospel. And he especially rejoiced because of the progress in the gospel. This common goal bound them together and kept the partnership working.

Paul kept reaching out farther and farther, possibly eventually to Spain, exposing himself to greater dangers in order to make Christ known. He expressed his concern that he could lose his life in the process. He was not afraid of death, but he realized that by staying alive he could still contribute to the growth and development of the Philippians so they could more perfectly share Christ as they "progress ... in the faith."

The mutual sharing of focused vision (3:1–16). One of the strongest bonds in Christian partnership is the sharing of a common goal. The power of mutually focused vision in Christian partnership is developed in chapter three.

First, focused vision attracts attention and commitment from others. Secondly, focused vision allows international partners to position themselves within their history and their own context. They are not intimidated. They establish trust in other Christian partners. They function with reliability. Thirdly, international partners with focused vision empower others as Paul did.

One of the hopes for the church in the West today is the spiritual empowerment that it can receive from the church in the Two-Thirds world as it seeks to empower the Two-Thirds world partners materially. Mutual empowerment comes when they have a mutual goal of advancing the gospel.

The foundation of a genuine Christian partnership — an association of two or more Christian autonomous bodies (1:12–24, 3:21).

Paul and Silas headed north, back into modern Turkey, with evidently no intentions of going on into Europe. But the "Macedonian call" changed their itinerary, and as a result, Paul developed one of the sweetest and most effective partnerships of his ministry.

Philippi, the leading city of Macedonia, came under the rule of a Roman proconsul, giving the people the protection and rights of Roman citizens. Nevertheless, Paul later described the Macedonian churches as suffering "extreme poverty" (2 Cor. 8:1–2).

As was his usual custom when arriving at a new city, Paul looked for a Jewish synagogue, but instead simply found a group of women praying by the river. One of them, Lydia, a businesswoman from Thyatira, was a devout seeker after God. She became Paul's first convert in Philippi, followed by the jailer and his family after Paul's miraculous release from prison, and then a slave girl who had been a fortune-teller.

Paul was able to return to visit Philippi at least twice on his journeys. The church, which by the time of the Philippian letter was large enough to have elders and deacons, developed a close, caring relationship with Paul. Though he loved all the churches dearly and prayed for them constantly, the Philippian church held a special place in his heart in spite of the insulting way he was treated in the city on his first visit.

Missiologist George Peters describes this partnership as follows:

Paul's partnership relationship was one of full participation in the life of the churches and in their mobilization and enlistment in prayer, personnel, and finances in evangelism. Paul discovered the resources for all his advances in evangelism and church expansion in the churches he planted. Thus the churches became involved with Paul from the very beginning in an aggressive program of evangelism and church multiplication ... it was a total partnership ministry from the very beginning.[2]

At the foundation of this Christian partnership, as at the foundation of any Christian partnership, was God himself, with emphasis on the second and third persons of the Godhead, the Lord Jesus Christ and the Holy Spirit.

To both Paul and the Philippian Christians the foundation of their partnership was none other than Christ himself (1:19–26). To Paul, life meant Christ. He could not think of life except in terms of Christ. The second chapter presents an inspired glimpse into the very nature of Jesus Christ. The four tremendous acts of God are captured as simple facts in the aorist tense of the Greek language: "He emptied Himself," (2:7); "He humbled Himself," (2:8); "God highly exalted Him, and gave Him a name that is above every name..." (2:9). These realities were foundational to every aspect of his life and ministry and thus were the common denominator in his partnership relationship. In fact, the application the apostle makes from this passage directly relates to Christian partnership — "to consider the other partner as more important than yourself."

In addition, as Paul begins to deal with some of the problems he has heard about in Philippi, he reminds them that their fellowship in the Spirit is their source of victory. Partnership in the Spirit can be represented by the "third strand" in a cord that is not easily broken. The Holy Spirit indwells all of them, and therefore is available for guidance, strength, wisdom, and comfort. The Holy Spirit purifies relationships and helps them make right decisions.

In letters to other churches, Paul spends a great deal of time explaining how to walk in the Spirit and to develop the fruits of the Spirit. In order to experience the blessings of the Spirit in this Philippian partnership, he urges them to submit themselves to the Spirit's control so that his joy would be complete.

Paul assumed that all members of the partnership could enjoy the benefits of the Spirit's influence. On the other hand, walking in the Spirit is a conscious effort that both Paul and the Philippians had to practice daily to maintain an intimate relationship and an effective ministry.

The philosophy of a genuine Christian partnership — sharing complementary strengths (1:2–1:11, 2:4–8, 3:20–21, 4:21)

Through the sharing of complementary gifts, each partner enables the other to grow. Each member in the Paul/Philippian relationship wanted the others to grow — to give the others opportunity, capacity, or means to fulfill their mission.

When Paul introduces himself to his partner church in Philippi, he does not use his normal identification tag. In the rest of his letters, with two exceptions, he identifies himself as Paul the Apostle, conveying the idea of his authority. To the Philippian partners he chooses to identify as a servant — a servant of Christ coming to be a servant of the Christians in Philippi.

He also plans to send Timothy to them, to encourage them and enable them to resolve some of their personal difficulties. Paul knows of no one else who will take such a genuine interest in their welfare (2:19–20). Timothy has served with Paul as a slave of Christ and has proven his value as one who knows how to enable others to grow.

Above all, Paul points to the supreme example of Christ who gave Himself completely to enable us to become like Him (3:21). Paul describes Jesus, the model servant, as the Enabler par excellence. From this model we can draw out some principles of enablement which apply to a healthy Christian partnership.

As described in Philippians, chapter 2, Jesus shows us that the empowerment of others is a matter of ambition, attitude, and action. First, empowerment involves the ambition to look after the interest of others, not only one's own interest (2:4). Secondly, empowerment is an attitude of ministry which involves thinking of the other as more important than oneself (2:5–8). Thirdly, empowerment is the action involving the giving of oneself for the sake of the partner. Empowerment gives and gives and gives again (2:5–8).

Paul states that partnership is a high calling involving the following:

- Look out for the interests of your partner (2:4)
- Develop a servant attitude (2:5–9)
- Continually give of yourself to meet the legitimate needs of your partner (2:8)
- Identify with your partner (2:7)
- Recognize that enablement is costly. You may have to renounce some of your own rights (2:8).

**The tangibles in the development of Christian partnerships —
a trusting relationship that fulfills agreed-upon expectations
by sharing resources (2:12–19, 1:9–10, 4:10–17)**

A trust relationship grows out of a properly formed partnership, for the ingredients of confidence are built into the initial understanding of each other's potential, and agreements of what each expects of the other. In a tangible way we might say that Christian partnership involves exchanging information for money.

Sharing the resource of ministry information (2:19, 1:9–10).
Epaphroditus brought information from the church to Paul, and
Timothy took information from Paul to the partner in Philippi.
Information is a precious resource. Living in an age called "the age of
information" we can certainly appreciate that fact today. Every
partnership calls for a transparent sharing of information of success
and failures in the overall task of advancing the gospel. Paul's honesty
in sharing information about his own ministry is evident throughout
the letter.

He excitedly reports to them that even though he is in prison, he
is able to tell people about Christ so that "the whole palace guard"
knows why he is there. And because of the unique prison arrangements of those days, many have heard from his own lips about the
Savior King. He wants them to know that their prayers and concern
have helped him reach their common goal.

In turn, he is sending Timothy to them. Paul has no doubt given
him a lot of verbal instructions and exhortations for them, but he also
wants to find out all the news from Philippi. He may have been
interested in who had gotten married, who had a baby, and who found
a new job.

Epaphroditus clearly was transparent in presenting to the Apostle
the problem of disunity that had arisen in the church, and Paul speaks
directly of that matter.

Accountability, as the flip side of trust, is built on the open
sharing of information. It is difficult to trust anyone who is unwilling
to be accountable, while it is humiliating to be accountable to someone
who does not trust us. Accountability is scriptural. No one could fault
Paul for honesty and integrity.

Financial partnership (4:10–17, 1:7). In Philippians Paul writes
frequently about money. He recognized (as he writes in chapter four)
what each Christian partner needs to recognize, that the ultimate
source of all supply is God Himself — that He is the Giver. In His own
purposes and wisdom, God has chosen to bless some individuals,
organizations, and societies with a relative abundance of funds and
holds them responsible as channels for His work. Ownership does not
rest with the steward. As funds are released for God's work, they
return to His control.

To most people partnership implies funding — usually the "haves"
funding the "have nots." A mission leader in the West complained,
"Since we control almost all the money, they [Two-Thirds world
churches and agencies] almost push us into positions of power
because we have it." On the other hand, a national development

leader expressed the quandary of Two-Thirds world organizations. "If a man has his hand in another man's pocket, he has to move when the other man moves."

The Philippians seemed to have learned financial partnering right from the earliest days of their relationship with Paul. But their financial obligation was mingled with love and concern as they sent their gifts with Epaphroditus so he could help in other ways and then report back the situation in which he found Paul.

Other churches took longer to learn their financial responsibilities, for Paul rather sadly confessed that other than the Philippians, "not one church shared with me in the matter of giving" (4:15).

Giving is often part of a chain reaction. Paul's Philippian partners sent funds to him for his needs as well as for others. Each gift resulted in thanksgiving to God and became an act of joyful fellowship.

Accountability does not imply mistrust. Accountability of time and money not only helps partners maintain trust but gives opportunity for rejoicing in God's work and provision.

The New Testament church grew and multiplied, taught and suffered, with little reference to trained leadership, budgets, and buildings. Money tends to cloud the issue of equality, since it too frequently becomes the dominant factor in a partnership. This, as in our biblical example, is something we must protect against with carefully-spelled-out financial policies and guidelines—and just as importantly, by taking on the more intangible responsibilities in the partnership.

The intangibles in a genuine Christian partnership form a trusting relationship (2:19–4:7)

Paul expressed his special love for the Philippians when he wrote to them, "I thank my God every time I remember you. In all my prayers for all of you, I always pray with joy because of your partnership in the gospel."

The intimacy of this special partnership is nowhere better reflected than in Paul's closing words, "Therefore, my brothers, you whom I love and long for, my joy and crown ... dear friends."

How was this intimacy maintained? How did they express their concern for one another? Three intangibles in the partnership—suffering, encouragement, and prayer—bonded them in love. These intangibles, rather than the tangible factors, held the structure together, providing the framework that gave the partnership shape.

Partnership in suffering (3:10). Paul wanted to know the fellowship of suffering with Christ. He was willing to pay whatever price was required to know and serve Christ fully. And he knew as he suffered, Christ would not forsake him.

While Paul could not add to the work of atonement, Ralph P. Martin in his commentary on Philippians states, "we must not evacuate the phrase of its rich meaning by taking it to mean simply that he shared his Lord's sufferings in imagination or sympathy."

Beaten or imprisoned, shipwrecked or shackled, Paul gladly suffered for Christ's sake, knowing His Savior had gone through much deeper suffering for him. Every pain helped him to better know and identify with the pains Christ endured for him.

Often, suffering for Christ is a lonely road, and nothing can be gained by simply volunteering to suffer with another for suffering's sake. Yet when we can fellowship in suffering by helping to alleviate the intensity, or supplying encouragement and fortitude in the pain, it is part of our commitment as partners.

The partnership of encouragement (2:19–30, 1:14). The church had heard of Paul's arrest in Jerusalem and wanted to encourage him. They picked one of their men who was perhaps an elder, named Epaphroditus, and sent him to assist Paul in his needs (2:25). Apart from bringing an offering, Epaphroditus remained with Paul and ministered to him, so much so that he himself became ill (2:25–30).

No partnership is perfect. Every partnership faces some kind of testing. Though Paul did not deal with a major sin in the Philippian church as he did in Corinth, or a serious doctrinal issue as in Galatia, he did intimate there were some areas that could cause problems.

Epaphroditus had evidently brought disturbing news of disunity in the Body. It might even have had to do with Paul, for he speaks of those who "preach Christ out of selfish ambition ... supposing that they can stir up trouble for me" (1:17). The fact that he wrote about this to the Philippians would indicate these people were either from Philippi or had passed through and were known to them.

Gently, tenderly, as a friend coming alongside a close friend, he enjoins, "then make my joy complete by being like-minded, having the same love, being one in spirit and purpose" (2:2). Paul encouraged unity in spirit and purpose.

There must have been a tremendous respect for each other's integrity for Paul to be able to counsel them in this way. A partnership that has built a strong relationship, as Paul and the Philippians had, can weather the problems that are bound to arise.

Partnering in prayer (4:5–7, 1:3–11, 1:19). This passage teaches that close human relationships and the motivation to pray are intricately interwoven. Paul's warmth of love and emotion pours itself out in fervent, frequent prayers of praise for what this partnership had meant to him. What must it have been like to listen in on those prayers of boundless joy as he brought this precious Body before the Lord?

No doubt he prayed for health, for safety and protection, for families and relationships. He must have longed for such personal news and must have plied Epaphroditus with dozens of questions when he arrived with their gift. Now he was planning to send Timothy to them for more information. Effectual prayer thrives on communication.

But Paul's prayers for his partners plumbed far greater depths than their personal health and welfare. He prayed that they would love more, learn more about spiritual truth, and gain discernment to make the right choices in their constant upward walk. Anticipating the time when their physical partnership would end, he taught them "in everything through prayer and petition with thanksgiving, present your requests to God" (4:6). Though for the present his enablement was so important for their growth that he preferred to stay in this life rather than go to be with Christ, he wanted them to be ready to trust that God alone could indeed "supply all their needs."

As in all good partnerships, benefits flow in two directions. Paul assured the Philippians that their prayers had been a great help and encouragement to him and that he believed they would effect his "deliverance."

Paul relates three things that were happening because of the partnership in prayer. First, though chained to a soldier day and night in four-hour shifts, the whole palace guard was being touched by his testimony. Secondly, he was comforted knowing that he had two sources of support—Jesus Christ himself and the prayers of the church (1:19). Thirdly, partner prayers would help Paul himself realize his own goals of speaking the truth in boldness as a privilege and a duty (1:20) and would insure that Christ be honored in his earthly life. One cannot build effective Christian partnerships without regular focused prayer.

Conclusion

Paul and the Philippians probably only met face to face three times over ten or twelve years. Their communications were limited to an occasional letter carried by hand over treacherous land and sea, or a rare visit from a mutual friend. Realizing this, we know that the bonding between them came from the Holy Spirit Himself. Eighteen centuries later, John Fawcett captured the ethos of this relationship in these words with which I close:

Blest be the tie that binds
Our hearts in Christian love;
The fellowship of kindred minds
Is like to that above.

Before our Father's throne
We pour our ardent prayers;
Our fears, our hopes, our aims are one,
Our comforts and our cares.

Endnotes

[1] Lausanne Committee for World Evangelization, *The Manila Manifesto: an Elaboration of the Lausanne Covenant, Fifteen Years Later,* (Pasadena, CA: Lausanne Committee for World Evangelization, 1989), 50.

[2] George Peters, *A Biblical Theology of Missions,* (Chicago: Moody Press, 1972), 234–35.

CHAPTER 2

The Context for Partnership

George Otis, Jr.

Abstract: *In the current rapidly changing world scene, success in ministry is dependent on our ability and willingness to adapt. Planning for effective missions must not only include a consideration for place — where are the unreached? — but also a consideration of timeliness — where are the windows of opportunity now open? A coordinated global prayer and communications effort to help discern where new "kairos"* opportunities for mission are opening is proposed.*

Introduction

"If the fingers of one hand quarrel, they cannot pick up the food." This East African proverb graphically expresses a weakness in world evangelization today.

Back in 1989, Paul McKaughan wrote in an article entitled "Cooperation and World Evangelization" that the great Achilles heel of world evangelization has been the unwillingness of the great spiritual entrepreneurs to lay aside their individualistic dreams and organizational manifestations and cooperate with others equally gifted and committed.

And in David Barrett and Jim Reapsome's *700 Plans to Evangelize the World*, we find a statistic equally revealing. Two-thirds of all those 700 plans for evangelism today are either not cooperating or only partially cooperating. Only 10.5 percent of those groups consider cooperation with like-minded traditions and bodies to be indispensable. This is astonishing.

---

*The word *kairos* is a Greek word for time which literally means ripened, mature, or full. A kairos opportunity is one that has "ripened." This concept is recalled in Mordecai's words to Esther, "Who knoweth whether thou art come to the kingdom for such a time as this?"

Extraordinary Challenges

If we take an in-depth look at Christian ministry today, we see extraordinary challenges. They range from the sheer numbers of the unreached to the geographical immensities to the cultural diversities to the furious pace at which change occurs. If we add to that the massive power of those who actively oppose efforts to proclaim the Gospel, the combined burden of all these factors can seriously impede the work of any one ministry. Only the added strength to be found in partnerships can bear up and advance under so much pressure.

Partnership Context

In discussing the matter of cooperation in ministry, it is useful to consider the context in which new partnerships will be required to operate in the mid-to-late 1990s. No arrangement ever operates in a vacuum, and the circumstances which surround us at any given time have a significant bearing on the number and types of our ministry relationships.

Much could be said on this topic but I want to confine my comments to the arena of change, and specifically, to the issue of where we are now on the continuum of history. Many believe we have recently entered a new season of divine initiative. This is the subject I hope to explore without trespassing into the field of eschatology.

Anyone who has followed the grand events of the late '80s and early '90s must realize the world they live and minister in today bears little resemblance to the world of 1988. History has taken not just one, but a series of sharp turns. We are living today in the midst of a meteor shower of change.

Today our success in ministry is predicated on our ability and willingness to adjust. The Evangelical Lutheran Church in America a few years ago made just such a course adjustment when they decided to strengthen significantly their witness to Muslims. At the time, one of their leaders, Dr. Mark Thomsen, observed: "If you can't adapt, then you might as well stay at home. A static church without the capacity to adapt is incapable of significant participation in the mission of God."

Several years ago in his book *The Church at the End of the Twentieth Century* (Downers Grove, Il: Inter-Varsity Press, 1970), Francis Schaeffer wrote: "Not being able, as times change, to change under the Holy Spirit is ugly. Refusal to consider change under the direction of the Holy Spirit is a spiritual problem, not an intellectual problem."

Fortunately, more and more Christian agencies these days are permitting the Holy Spirit to have His way. Major adjustments in prevailing attitudes and structures are having an impact on everything from interministry cooperation to ministry methods and the setting of priorities. Regarding this latter issue, priorities, there is truth in the old maxim that success comes from being in the right place at the right time. Regarding this issue of "*placeness*," if I might be permitted to coin a term, we have come to understand that some places are more strategic than others when it comes to deploying resources. To warrant fresh attention and resources today, a harvest field must qualify by being one of the following:

- an underserviced or neglected people
- an area of extraordinary harvest
- a *kairos* opportunity

Strategic Placeness

Over the past few years, a number of mission leaders have drawn our attention to a grossly neglected area of the world now referred to as "the 10/40 window." As the decade began, we were shocked to learn that within this area encompassing North Africa, Central Asia, and pockets of the Far East, one could find more than 95 percent of the world's unreached peoples. Accordingly, in terms of strategic placeness, the lands and peoples of the 10/40 window have become exceedingly important to us.

Extraordinary Harvests

Strategic placeness also encompasses what, for lack of a better term, I call extraordinary harvests. Whereas kairos openings create the *contextual opportunities* for lucrative evangelism, extraordinary harvests are places where large numbers of people are already being brought into the Kingdom. While "normal" spiritual harvesting is going on in one place or another on a more or less consistent basis, extraordinary harvests are, by contrast, rare events (although in recent years they are becoming less so). Whenever these spectacular harvests are reported, partnerships must be formed to help our local brothers and sisters bring in their treasure.

Strategic Timeliness

Being in the right place, however, is not the only ingredient for ministry success. In addition to the idea of strategic placeness, God is now wanting to tutor His Church in the concept of *strategic timeliness*. In addition to ascertaining windows of *need* such as the 10/40 window, He is also asking Christians to pay attention to windows of *opportunity*.

While the phenomenon of kairos opportunities is certainly nothing new, only the exceptional individual could have imagined the pace or the dimensions of the events that have visited the end of the twentieth century. Based on the available evidence, it would appear that God has been at work "redeeming" heavenly vials of vintage intercession (see Revelation, chapters 5 and 8).

Not long ago I had the privilege of spending four days with a group of real spiritual heroes — nearly 25 Arab Christian leaders who had gathered in Europe from nations throughout the Middle East and North Africa. A year had passed since I had last seen them, and they were ripe with stories of what God had done during this brief period.

As the accounts came in — from Iraq, Egypt, Lebanon, Algeria, and Saudi Arabia — all of us were struck by the way God had redemptively used the Gulf War tragedy to pry open unprecedented windows of ministry opportunity in the Middle East.

In Saudi Arabia, for instance, we heard how years of inhospitality to the Gospel had recently given way to an outpouring of the Holy Spirit. Hundreds of Saudi Muslims were reported to have been drawn to Christ in the early months of 1991 alone. In war-torn Iraq, the harvest was even greater. Among the many exciting reports coming out of that country were accounts of young Republican Guards being saved in military convoys, and highly fruitful ministry programs among the Kurds near the city of Kirkuk. A believer conscripted into Saddam Hussein's army was delivered from execution at the hands of the dreaded military police in the Basra area so that he could return to ministry in Baghdad.

Although time, space, and security considerations prevent me from sharing all of these remarkable stories, I can report that none of the Arab believers I spoke to in Europe had ever before witnessed such a brilliant bouquet of ministry opportunities. All sensed that the region was entering a new season of divine initiative.

The story is the same elsewhere. In Asia dramatic openings have occurred in reclusive Mongolia, the killing fields of Cambodia, and in the Hindu kingdom of Nepal. In Eastern Europe we are astonished by

the large-scale evangelistic rallies being held in such places as the
Soviet Union and Albania.

Anticipate the Harvest

As we help the church in these areas muscle their newly-laden
spiritual nets into the boat, however, several puzzling questions arise.
Why, for instance, was the Body of Christ not better prepared for these
exceptional harvests? Did we not see them coming? Had God
presented us with early indicators that we failed to detect? Can we
find a way to enhance our ability to anticipate and respond to
emerging windows of opportunity in the future?

When asked the secret of his success, the Canadian hockey star
Wayne Gretzky once replied: "I can anticipate where the hockey puck
will be and get there before it does." No preacher could come up with
a better description of what the church must do if it is to take advantage
of kairos opportunities in the coming years.

Knowing where tomorrow's windows of opportunity will occur,
and how long they are likely to remain open, is of vital importance to
the Church in the 1990s. If we can detect *where* God is going to move
next, we can then mobilize and pre-position resources for ministry. If
we can determine *how long* an opportunity is going to last, we can
establish an appropriate strategy. For example, knowing whether we
have two months or twenty years has a profound bearing on the
approach to ministry we are likely to take. In the absence of such a time
frame, our strategic decisions amount to little more than guesswork.
(Wouldn't it be helpful to know how much longer Christians will be
able to conduct open ministry in the Soviet Union?)

While such knowledge is undeniably useful, the real question is
whether it is obtainable. If it is, there has never been a better time for
it. In the past, windows of ministry opportunity may have emerged
once every few centuries. Today they are opening up at a rate of three
or four per year. I believe this has to do with the fact that more
Christians are praying today than ever before. As of 1990, an estimated 30 million believers were praying regularly for world evangelization—many of them as participants in one of 10 million weekly
prayer meetings or 2,400 international prayer networks.

With this many Christians addressing heaven on the subject of
world evangelization, we might ask what exactly is God sharing with
His Church? While we may be able to discern what He is saying to us
personally, or perhaps even what His word is for our church, ministry,

or denomination, do we have any idea what He is saying to the global Body of Christ? While this "big picture" may not have meant as much two or three decades ago, the internationalization of today's mission force along with a rapidly changing battlefield has made it an essential ingredient of ministry success.

It is into this context that my own ministry, the Sentinel Group, is now preparing to introduce the **Global Prayer Harvest** program — an effort to harvest and scrutinize systematically the results of prayer sessions around the world. The program assumes that God is providing advance information to His Church concerning emerging windows of ministry opportunity, but that this information is not being adequately recorded or shared with leaders.

Every three to four months Sentinel will gather standardized reports from prayer networks on every continent. The information contained in these reports will then be fed into a computer to look for significant patterns and emphases. For example, if a future prayer harvest were to reveal that God was prompting multiple prayer groups in Brazil, Korea, Egypt, and Norway to intercede for spiritual breakthroughs in Somalia, could this not represent an early indicator of Divine intervention?

If this kind of spiritual seismograph had been in place in the mid-1980s, I am convinced it would have provided substantial evidence concerning impending changes in Eastern Europe. Given this assumption, would we not therefore have been better prepared to launch our ministry partnerships at the appropriate moment?

Why is this so important? In light of the fact that Christian churches and agencies often take considerable time to gear up their response to new opportunities, and that many windows do not remain open for more than a few months or years, failure to anticipate these openings often results in their being missed altogether. Unfortunately, history is littered with these sad stories.

Several years ago I read about Kublai Khan, the nephew of Ghengis Khan, who ruled over the largest human empire this world has ever known. Once when he was visited by Marco Polo in China, the great Khan issued a request that Polo prevail upon the Pope to send Christian missionaries to the Mongol kingdom. Kublai Khan would then grant them permission to itinerate throughout his great empire and talk to people about the Gospel. The Church's response? Two semi-literate priests were finally dispatched to the Middle Kingdom only to return home shortly after their arrival — an opportunity sadly lost.

Consider the meek response to the call for missionaries in post-World War II Japan—another example of an open window since closed by widespread materialism and non-Christian religions like Sokka-gakkai. Japan is now a tough place to work. A more recent missed opportunity involved God's desire to redeem the tragedy of the Soviet invasion of Afghanistan; an apocalypse which sent 5 million needy Afghan Muslims spilling over their borders. Many of these souls fled into Pakistan where they were more easily accessible to Christian ministry.

Unfortunately, with the exception of a few stalwart organizations like SERVE, the Church really missed an opportunity there. Despite the fact that missions strategists were reminding us that Afghanistan represented one of the most restricted nations on the face of the earth, we could not see our way forward. Somehow we failed to predict that maybe God would permit the Afghans to come to us.

To break out of this syndrome, we need to develop effective anticipatory mechanisms, and then move on to create the equivalent of a spiritual emergency response system and rapid deployment teams. In other words, we must not only be able to detect emerging windows of ministry opportunity, we must be able to respond as well.

Partnerships are needed today among local churches and agencies who are "lightly packed" (unencumbered with restrictive policies and infrastructure) or who are willing to develop and maintain the equivalent of a rapid deployment force within their overall structure—some part of their whole that could be released to quickly respond to windows of opportunity as they open up. These teams could be comprised of spiritually mature, cross-culturally experienced personnel who could be deployed into emerging situations to establish a foothold of ministry until they were reinforced by more substantial or permanent resources.

That such international rapid deployment partnerships are needed was evidenced by the recent openings in Kuwait. As this war-torn nation began to rebuild its infrastructure, it sought to bring in a labor force from around the world. In addition to labor from the West, the Kuwaitis were looking to nations such as Pakistan, Egypt, and the Philippines where large numbers of Christians are found. If we network together in partnership, when these kinds of opportunities open up information can be quickly disseminated allowing for a rapid strategic Christian response.

Conclusion

Finally, we would do well to draw more outside disciplines into our missiological fraternity. When it comes to developing our observational and anticipatory skills, we need to be sharpened through partnerships with Christians in governmental, academic, business, and secular media circles. I have had many valuable and enlightening conversations with people in such positions over the past several years. I only wish I had made a habit of this sooner. I'm afraid that we often exclude these people as resources because they are not "of us." We are too much a closed shop. As a consequence, we miss out on contacts and information that could help us.

"... the men of Issachar understood the times, and knew what Israel should do." (I Chronicles 12:32)

"Go set a watchman. Let him declare what he sees." (Isaiah 21:6)

Additional information on this subject is contained in Mr. Otis' book, *The Last of the Giants*, published by Chosen Books, Tarrytown, NY, 1991. For more information contact: The Sentinel Group, P.O. Box 6334, Lynnwood, WA, 98036 USA.

Section 2

❖❖❖

Integrated Partnerships

CHAPTER 3

Why Strategic Partnerships? A Look At New Strategies for Evangelism

Phill Butler

Abstract: *The global context and our desire, as stewards, for effectiveness demand new forms and structures for ministry. The Scriptures point to partnership and functional community as a model for effective witness. Interdev's mission includes facilitating "vertically integrated partnerships": voluntary strategic alliances that bring churches and agencies together for coordinated ministry to a particular language group or context.*

A Partnership Story

High in the Atlas mountains of North Africa, in a small village, lived a young Muslim by the name of Aziz. This young man provided for his widowed mother and siblings, sustaining them with the earnings of a small shop he managed.

Aziz became increasingly disillusioned with Islam, with the impossibility of continuing his education, and with other factors in his life. So, late at night he began to listen to Christian radio programs and became fascinated by this person called Jesus Christ. After listening for a number of months he wrote a letter to the producers. They wrote back. And then began a flow of letters that continued for months.

Eventually, the producers suggested that Aziz might like to get involved in Bible correspondence courses. They did not offer Bible correspondence courses, but (and this is a key point) they knew a group that did.

So Aziz enrolled. He found it tough work, running the shop all day making income for his family, completing the courses, and listening to radio programs at night, but he persevered. After a couple of years of working through two or three courses, he finally penned these words to the people with whom he corresponded: "I would really like to meet someone who is a believer in Jesus."

That trigger kicked off contact by a Moroccan national evangelist associated with yet another organization known to the correspondence course people. The evangelist had tea with Aziz. In fact, they continued to have contacts over a considerable period of time. And eventually this young man opened his heart to the Lord Jesus Christ.

Subsequently he was passed on to a so-called tentmaker, an expatriate who lived in the town, and this person began a process of discipleship with Aziz.

Now, the moral of this story is quite clear: the individual parts of Christ's Body had combined to do something that none of them could do separately. What we have here is an integration of four or five different ministries linking hands in succession, accomplishing different parts of a process; the process of sowing, watering, reaping, and eventually discipling. This was a conscious, intentional integration of the body of Christ for a specific objective.

Introduction to Integrated Partnerships

I want to talk about partnerships specifically within the context of frontier missions, focusing on those people who have never had an opportunity to hear the good news. I believe strongly that the idea of partnership touches on many different aspects of human affairs and has relevance to all aspects of Kingdom life. It is relevant, of course, to the existing church in areas where the gospel of Christ may have been known for millennia. But our focus at Interdev derives primarily out of a call to the "unreached people" or the great two billion, plus or minus, who have not yet heard.

I am addressing myself primarily to people groups, regional areas, or megacities where presently no significant indigenous witness exists. I am not talking about most of sub-Sahara Africa, Europe, the European part of the Soviet Union, or even Latin America. I am talking about those areas which are primarily Hindu, Islamic, Buddhist, or Tibetan Buddhist.

When William Carey stepped off the boat in 1783 in Calcutta, he was one man facing an entire subcontinent. Now, there you have a generalist *en extremis*. In contrast, today's Christian context offers an extraordinary range of specialties, or diversity of witness. The full flowering of St. Paul's imagery of the body of Christ may be more vivid and relevant today than at any other time in the history of the Church. With today's diverse forms of witness and service, the eyes, hands, arms, and the feet seem more obvious than ever.

The whole world, it seems, is full of talk about partnerships and strategical alliances. Partnership has become a buzz word in the church in the last few years. But in business and industry as well, strategic alliances have been a hot topic—and the basis for major working strategies.

The lead article in the *International Executive Digest* a few months ago highlighted strategic alliances. The recent best-selling book, *Partnerships for Profit*, by Wharton School of Business professor Jordan Lewis, focuses on structuring and managing strategic alliances. And recently *Business Tokyo*, a journal of international business for executives in Japan, had as its lead article, "Strategical Alliances." We have seen only the beginning of this theme of partnering for greater effectiveness.

In this conference we are exploring partnerships in a number of specific contexts; like church to church, mission to mission, north-south-east-west, and Two-Thirds world to Two-Thirds world. We will look at some general principles and then some particulars in specific illustrations—some nitty-gritty details about what it takes to make partnerships work. But despite this effort at detail, I acknowledge in advance that in the space allotted, I am treating the subject with some superficiality.

I want to acknowledge the essential importance of church to church, mission to mission, north-south-east-west, and Two-Thirds world to Two-Thirds world partnerships. However, Interdev, for the last six years, has focused on another kind of partnership which, at least until recently, has not had much attention. This is a well known type of partnership in business and industry. It is frequently found in social marketing campaigns and a range of other applications. But in the church it really did not see the light of day until recent years.

Horizontal and Vertical Integration

Following from the story of Aziz, I would like to show one or two illustrations from industry. Businesses are frequently identified as being integrated one of two ways, either horizontally or vertically.

Let's look at the plastics industry—a very sophisticated industry starting with petrochemicals, engineering people, and PhDs. This includes all kinds of basic research, marketing people, industrial process people, and distribution personnel. They produce international symposia, and all kinds of papers, monographs, and journals. Plastics can be applied to a wide range of industries. But in the end, it is still just plastics. No matter how sophisticated, no matter how complex, it is only plastics. It is a *horizontally* integrated industry (see Figure 3.1).

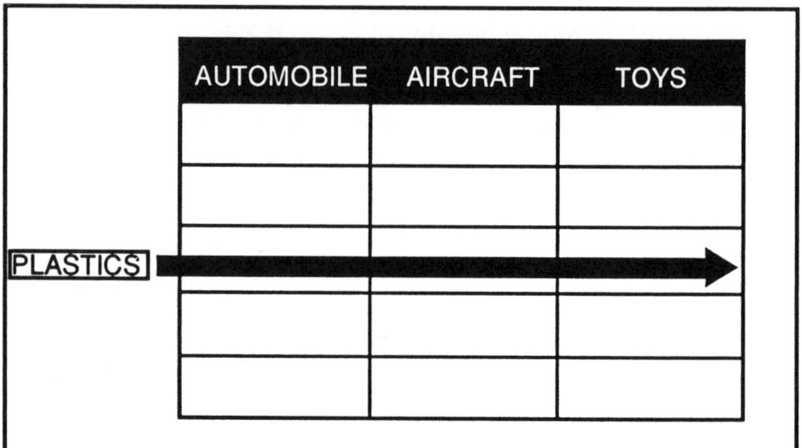

	AUTOMOBILE	AIRCRAFT	TOYS
PLASTICS →			

An industry like plastics may "horizontally" serve a wide range of other business applications.

Figure 3.1

By contrast, if I go out in the parking lot and examine a Ford Escort, I am now faced with another form of integration. If I want to build a Ford Escort, I cannot use only plastics. I must integrate steel, electronics, plastics, rubber, computers, industrial design—all of those elements have to be *vertically* integrated for a single objective, the construction of an automobile (see Figure 3.2).

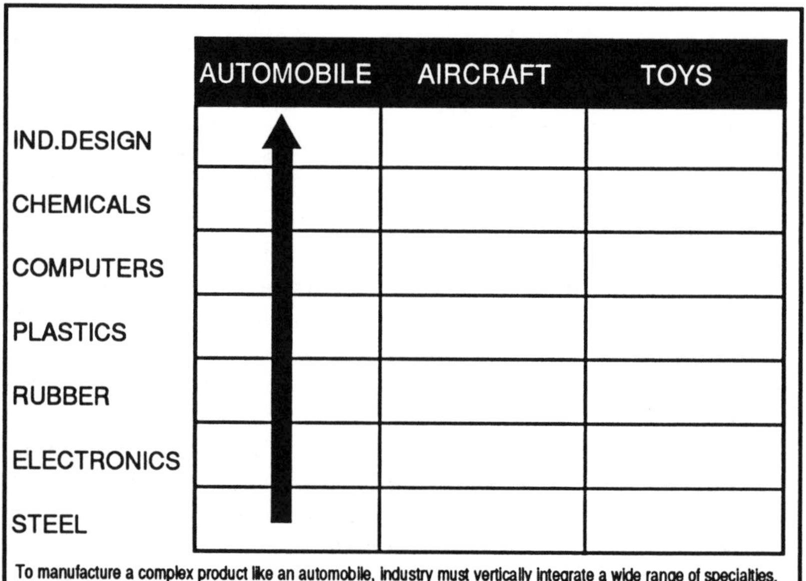

	AUTOMOBILE	AIRCRAFT	TOYS
IND.DESIGN	↑		
CHEMICALS			
COMPUTERS			
PLASTICS			
RUBBER			
ELECTRONICS			
STEEL			

To manufacture a complex product like an automobile, industry must vertically integrate a wide range of specialties.

Figure 3.2

Now how does this relate to Kingdom affairs and the matter of partnership? Let's take a look at three mythical unreached people groups: the Olongos, the Dubis, and the Zawads. One specialty, such as broadcasting, may be serving all three of these language groups. But if we want to see the church of Jesus Christ built among the Olongos, according to St. Paul's definition, we must integrate Scripture translation, medical work, broadcasting development, literature, visiting teams, and personal witness into a conscious, intentional, vertically-integrated, voluntary partnership built on Kingdom principles (see Figure 3.3).

	OLONGOS	DUBIS	ZAWADS
PERSONAL WITNESS			
VISITING TEAMS			
LITERATURE			
BROADCASTING			
DEVELOPMENT			
MEDICAL			
SCRIPTURE TRANSLATION			

Broadcasting (or any other specialty) may "horizontally" serve a wide range of language groups. However in a single unreached language group (like the Olongos above) the objective of seeing a viable national church is most likely when all the specialties are "vertically" integrated into a coordinated strategy.

Figure 3.3

This is no longer just William Carey, one man against a subcontinent. What we really see here is an imperative placed on us by the Scripture. We are called on by God as good stewards to orchestrate the elements of the body of Christ into a coordinated strategy for maximum return on investment.

Interdev and the partner agencies with whom we are now working are absolutely committed to the essential nature of *both* horizontal and vertical networks or integration. The horizontal networks are critical, for example, in scripture translation. Without that world of

PhDs and linguistic analysis, international papers and monographs, and the training programs that the Summer Institute of Linguistics sponsors, we would not have the modern linguistic Scripture translation movement.

That *horizontal* network ties people together across nationalities, across languages, and across continents. It makes Scripture translation functional and able to serve the Olongo people group. But Scripture translation, by itself, is only one part of the group of Kingdom assets needed to reach the Olongos.

If church to church, east-west-north-south, mission to mission, and Two-Thirds world to Two-Thirds world partnerships are to play their vital roles, all of these specialized forms of partnership need to ultimately find expression in a local language group or context. They must find their expression finally in some kind of integrated, specific, coordinated strategy bringing the various elements of the body of Christ together. So a strategic partnership, locally or regionally focused, will ultimately maximize the return on the Kingdom investments that we and others make (see Figure 3.4).

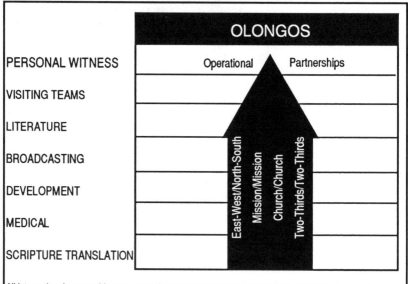

Figure 3.4

Partnerships and Community

One issue has not yet received much attention. I am not a missiologist—my degree is in Business Administration. But for 30 years I have been around the so-called "last great frontiers" of missions—Hinduism, Islam, Buddhism, Tibetan Buddhism, and others. I am amazed that only *occasionally* in brief comments in anthropological journals and in missiological journals do I hear much about the number one social value which towers above all other values in these cultures.

What is it?

Community, of course. Relationships. It is how you stand with your father. The extent to which your father is in good standing with his brothers. The extent to which your family is thought well of in the community. The extent to which you honor the caste or the tribe, depending on what particular religious group you are talking about.

We will never see a viable reproducing church in traditional cultures until we can present them an alternative community which is equal to or better than the community we ask them to leave. But how can we present an alternative community to these last great frontiers of unreached people when we are presenting Christ in a fragmented, individualistic way?

I confess my sins. As a product of Western society I know precious little about living in community. But I can tell you this. Over the last seven years, as we have been trying to encourage people to come to grips with restoration of relationships and building functional communities in partnership, I have been increasingly convinced of its absolutely critical nature. And of the fact that it can and does happen.

I remember a circumstance some time ago where sixteen men in one partnership came to a working meeting to try and iron out some extremely challenging but practical matters. At the outset, their mistrust and fear of each others' backgrounds could be easily sensed. The going was tough.

However, after three days of intensive prayer and work together, two things occurred. First, they hammered out detailed, working arrangements that have allowed their ministries to cooperate effectively up to the present—the result being many more people in that region making inquiry about Christ and being effectively followed up.

Second, when they came to the end of the meeting these men shared communion together and embraced, many in tears, and went away with a whole new sense of fellowship, trust, and commitment to each other.

These working partnerships are not just a theoretical witness, but a functional witness to the glorious healing and transforming nature of God. Above all else, the good news of the Lord Jesus Christ is good news about transformed relationships — not a list of theological facts. Jesus when confronted by the young attorney who asked, "How may I gain eternal life?" said, "Love God, love yourself, and love your neighbor. Do that and you're home free." But of course, it is impossible outside of Christ and the power of the Holy Spirit to do that.

Encapsulated, the story of the gospel is transformed, restored relationships. Unless we can live this in operational partnerships on the field, we have nothing to say to these last great community-driven cultures.

Biblical Rationale for Partnerships

A strong Biblical mandate supports partnerships. First, *God's character is the source of community and cooperation*. Before the world was created, God was living in fellowship with other beings. Because he creates in kind and is always true to himself, it follows that he would create man in his own image — to live and work in relationship, in community.

In the book of Genesis, multiple times in the first eleven chapters, God refers to himself in the *plural*. Read the books of Daniel, Job, Ephesians. Again and again we see the words about the principalities and powers in heavenly places and the angels and other forces looking down. They are interacting with the sons of men in what is obviously a cosmic process — not just a time-and history-bound process.

So, community, relationships, how we operate in the field — these are born out of the character of God. This is not something we learn from secular models (though they frequently confirm the truth). This is not driven by anthropology and sociology but rather by God's character.

Second, Paul gives what I like to call the integrated assets model in Romans 12, 1 Corinthians 12, and Ephesians 4 — *the body of Christ working as the orchestrated function of all the different, Spirit-inspired parts*. Partnerships allow these varied, God-given elements to consciously function together for Christ's glory.

Now let's look at a third aspect to the Biblical mandate for partnerships. From Genesis to Revelation *two levels of communication are outlined in Scripture*. From beginning to end we see clearly that there is *individual witness*, exemplified by a legion of personalities. But equally clearly there runs throughout Scripture what I believe to be the primary form of witness—*community witness*. This form towers above the other and is the principal validation of individual witness.

For example, when God made his promise to Abraham in Genesis, he did not say He would make him happy, wealthy, or bright, as an individual. No, He said, "I am going to make you a great nation." In Nehemiah when Israel was being carted off into captivity and brought back, the nations stood in awe. They laughed when Israel was captured and then stood in awe and wondered as God restored the nation. Israel was a community witness to a community of nations. Jesus' high priestly prayer raises the same issue when he suggests that our relationships are the telltale indicator of authenticity to the community around us.

A fourth level of concern in the Scripture mandating partnership is the fact that *the Holy Spirit of God is only released when God's people dwell in unity.*

We frequently wonder why we do not see the power of God breaking through in the last great bastions of darkness. Could it be because we are living in dissension and fragmentation? Psalm 133 states that the Holy Spirit of God rests only where God's people dwell in unity.

And functional partnerships give us the practical opportunity to deal with the "nuts and bolts" of working unity. At Interdev, we have never yet seen a partnership come together because people first met to talk about unity. This never happens. We come together regarding functional, practical issues, and as work progresses effectively on these issues, trust and unity begin to emerge.

A fifth Scriptural reason also indicates why partnerships strategies are critical at the grassroots level. Jesus said that the *credibility of the Gospel* is established by how we work together. A large portion of what we actually say is what we do.

Frequently we just want to give our audience a litany of theological truths, a cognitive experience. Now, remarkably, some people do respond to that type of message and their lives are transformed. Praise God, it has happened millions of times. But a desire for real effectiveness requires we listen to the mandate of the Scripture. Jesus says, "The world has every right to say, 'Ah ha, you're a fake,' if they don't see my followers living and working together in unity."

Communications Experience Points to Partnership

It is not just the Biblical mandate that commends partnership. Our experience in communications for evangelism also demonstrates the need for cooperation. If we take, for example, mass media at one end of the continuum and interpersonal, face-to-face communication at the other end, we see that they are *both* needed for effective witness, especially as we come to the decision-making point in the conversion process (see Figure 3.5).

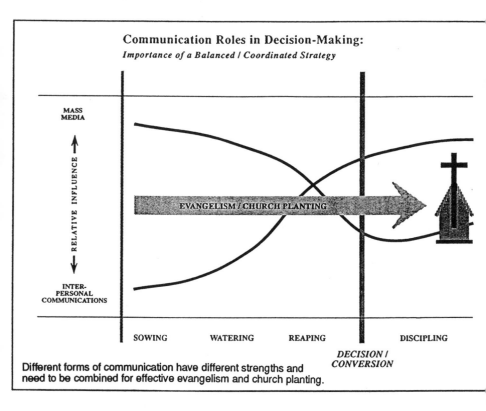

Figure 3.5

Consider Jesus' metaphors of sowing, watering, reaping, and discipling. Both social communication theory and the practical work done in the field make clear that as one approaches the decision or conversion point, the effectiveness of the mass media declines and the importance of interpersonal communication rises.

This is generally true in decisions that have serious social implications. And we certainly know that coming to Christ in a traditional Islamic, Hindu, or Tibetan Buddhist society has significant social implications. It is therefore absolutely crucial, if we want to see people come into the Kingdom, that we have a coordinated, integrated working relationship.

World Trends and Partnerships

However, it is not just biblical mandate or communication practice that commends partnership. World conditions mandate cooperation as well. We are faced not only with a new day of enhanced communications and widely distributed economic and technical resources, but new demands all over the world call for heightened efficiency.

If we read *Fortune* or *International Business Week* or any one of a half-dozen international business journals, we see industry worldwide down-sizing in terms of size of staff and out-sourcing through outside vendors. At the same time industry is being forced to increase profits. Now, are we down-sizing and out-sourcing in missions while, at the same time, increasing return for the Kingdom?

But there is even more at stake than demand for efficiency. According to UNESCO, population trends indicate the highest growth rates correlate with those areas that are most resistant to the Gospel.

For instance, UNESCO indicates that the Soviet Union in 58 years is going to grow by roughly 100 million people, 85 million of those in Islamic areas. This suggests that by the year 2050, Muslims will be a majority in the Soviet Union. These things might keep us awake at night because of the imagination they fire in us. But in any case, we have to deal with rapidly changing circumstances.

Mission Agency Motivation for Partnership

But beyond all these reasons, concerned and effective missions leaders have plenty of motivations for considering active involvement in partnerships.

First, we all want to build on existing strengths, and we all do have existing strengths. Those may be our people, technical facilities, our regional specialties, or our special experience. So as an administrator or a leader of a missions agency, I would want to know my ministry's strengths and build on those, not reinventing the wheel or duplicating some other agency's work.

Secondly, despite commitments to frontier areas acknowledged to be high risk, I would want to reduce my risks as much as possible. We reduce risks when we join hands with other ministries.

Finally, as a mission leader, partnerships should be attractive to me for another reason. By linking up with other ministries, I can consider service in new areas that would be impossible if my ministry tried to "go it alone." Sharing the risk, costs, and advance work through a partnership can significantly expand my ministry's potential to consider new areas of service.

Partnership Precedents in Missions

Precedents in the field of partnerships for evangelism include well-known ones like United Mission to Nepal, International Assistance Mission, ACROSS in southern Sudan, and HEED Bangladesh.

These partnerships were motivated by a variety of circumstances. In some cases it was the necessity of uniting to present a single face to a hostile government. In other cases groups desired to link certain specialties for functional reasons. However, in no case that I know of prior to around 1980, was there an effort made to form an evangelism partnership *intentionally* uniting the various ministries necessary for a comprehensive, vertically-integrated approach.

Current Opportunities and The Future

More recently, partnerships focusing on specific language groups date back to about 1985. Today, to our knowledge, seven of these partnerships operate with 100–130 partner agencies involved. It is good news that about 35 percent of these partner ministries are non-Western. Some of the partnerships are made up of 100 percent national or Two-Thirds world agencies. In addition to these seven operational partnerships, probably another five or six are in various stages of formation — and perhaps another ten or twelve are being discussed.

However, we find it remarkable at Interdev that virtually every month another serious opportunity arises to develop an initiative along these lines. Experienced field personnel, challenged by some unreached people group and aware of significant resources are saying, "Can you help us develop a response to this opening?"

Clearly tremendous opportunities confront us. And we are learning significant things. One thing we have learned is this — you do not start a partnership by calling a meeting. That is likely the quickest way to kill a partnership.

We have learned that forming partnerships takes time—lots of time. Most partnerships with which we are involved have taken from one to three years of quiet, patient work and endless discussions.

One recent partnership involved my travel to ten countries, personally talking with the senior leadership of more than thirty mission societies. It would be impossible to tell you of the dozens (maybe even hundreds) of phone calls, faxes, and informal discussions over a period of three years before the first official meeting was called. But to have called a meeting too early could have dealt a death blow to a partnership covering about six million people.

We are also finding out things about partnership structures. For example, we prefer consensus-based partnerships over constitutional partnerships. We understand the value in constitutionality in places that necessitate such action. Sometimes a legal entity is needed to carry on protocol with the government.

But in most cases, constitutional structures are not needed, and they tend to get in the way more than they facilitate God's people coming together. The likelihood of developing strong interpersonal relationships is largely a function of the ability to work in consensus rather than depending on constitutional rights.

We are learning about what kind of people are required to lead partnerships. No partnership will ever function without a person committed 110% to the ongoing life of the partnership. Partnerships do not spontaneously happen, nor are they spontaneously maintained. They require unrelenting commitment day after day, night after night, month after month, on the part of someone totally committed to the idea of cooperation.

We now see a pattern developing and think it best if that leader is an outside third-party person; not a Scripture translator, nor a radio broadcaster, nor a tentmaker. This person needs to be able to play an independent role assisting and facilitating all sides of the partnership. This coordinator of the partnership is constantly switching hats—one day wearing a prophet hat, the next day a servant hat, and so forth.

We are learning much about the difficulties. One of the biggest trouble spots arises when the members try to write out a theological statement. Basically we have found four main characteristics of partnerships that breed insensitivity.

- Lack of proper training for the leadership
- Partner agency expectations (they all have their own constituencies)
- Partnerships tend to take on a personality all their own
- The goals are too grandiose

The big question is, as we learn how to develop and sustain these types of working partnerships for evangelism, how can we multiply them rapidly?

In response to that, Interdev, in cooperation with a number of other mission agencies, has been working for some time on a training program for Strategic Partnership Coordinators. Starting early next month, we expect more than twenty individuals from about ten countries and 14–15 ministries to gather for the first of these training sessions. Based in the United Kingdom, this two-week intensive course will focus on starting and maintaining effective partnerships.

Based on what is learned in that program, we are planning one or two such training programs each year in different parts of the world. The whole point is to empower our missions community with the practical skills needed to multiply and sustain the partnership vision.

Conclusion

In summary, the nature of mission has and continues to change. World conditions and our desire, as stewards, for effectiveness demand new structures for work and ministry.

The Scriptures have consistently pointed to partnership and functional community as a model for effective witness. In both the Church and the world of business, there is much talk of partnership and strategic alliances. And in missions, we are gaining an increasing amount of experience in working partnerships. Overall, that experience has been encouraging and suggests that much more can and should be done.

Clearly tremendous opportunities exist for those with vision and courage. Through working partnerships, we believe it is possible to reach these last great frontiers, effectively using Kingdom resources and convincingly communicating with resistant, traditional cultures. We pray that God will raise up men and women with the faith, patience, and tenacity that viable partnerships require.

CHAPTER 4

Strategic Partnership: A Case Study

Keith M. Fraser-Smith

Abstract: *This case study details the development, structure, and strengths and weaknesses of a vertically integrated regional partnership whose purpose is to facilitate church planting and growth in an unreached area.*

Introduction

As I arrived at the Holiday Inn for these meetings, I was looking through the Far West Suburban telephone directory and decided to look at the kinds of churches. There I discovered seventy different categories of churches in this area, and eleven of these were various kinds of Baptist churches. This may give us some idea of the problems involved in trying to work together.

I was attending an important meeting of national Christians and Western missionaries in a European capital to which I had travelled overnight by bus from London. The subject was Bible translation.

We had been discussing a fairly detailed contract to be signed between two of the parties present. Hearing the national brothers share their vision and their conditions, I could see no way that they were going to sign the document. Then one of them suddenly said, "But isn't this a partnership?" The representative of the translation agency exclaimed, "But our mission has never been involved in a partnership before."

This highlights just one of the difficulties facing the Western missionary society as it enters into meaningful partnership with Two-Thirds world mission agencies. The West crosses its "t's" and dots its "i's", preferring contracts to vulnerable relationships of trust.

This paper describes an active Regional or Integrated Partnership. For security reasons the name of the partnership will not be mentioned as it operates within the 10/40 window, a spiritually resistant region of the world to which access is restricted by traditional missionary methods.

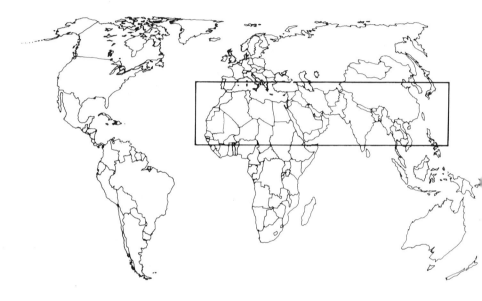

A Strategic Evangelism Partnership in the 10/40 Window

Figure 4.1

This Regional or Integrated Partnership will simply be referred to as the Strategic Evangelism Partnership (SEP). SEP is a major regional cooperative effort which brings together a young emerging national church, national agencies, and expatriate missions.

The purpose of the partnership is to facilitate church planting and growth among the peoples of the region. This paper will describe the history, the activities, and the decision-making procedures of the partnership. The presentation ends with an evaluation of the Regional Partnership.

History

Since 1986, a number of ministries have been meeting in an effort to more closely coordinate and increase the effectiveness of their ministry to the target area. The background for such an initiative came from a long association of the radio ministries in the region with the Seattle-based organization called Interdev (International Development Organization).

The initial group of some eight Partner Agencies (PA) has now grown to twenty.

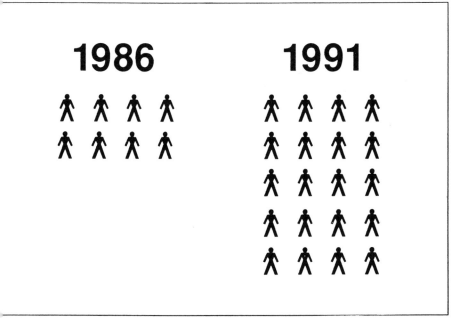

Figure 4.2

This group is comprised of:

- Western mission agencies of two varieties: Western only and those which include Two-Thirds world members
- Two-Thirds world mission agencies
- European-based national agencies from the region
- Representatives of the national church

SEP is a voluntary fellowship of like-minded agencies and has sought to embrace any ministry concerned with seeing Christ's Church established in the region. The PA play a variety of roles in the region from media, through tentmaking, to specialist ministries.

In addition to large coordination meetings, specialized working groups and functional projects are underway. A Review and Planning Meeting (R/PM) is held annually among the senior leaders of the PA. Some PA have both media and on-the-ground (OTG) ministries and they are represented by two or more members.

The Review and Planning Meeting (R/PM)

The Review and Planning meeting embraces all the PA, and it is the focus of the partnership's activities. At this annual meeting, normally held in January, the previous year's activities are reviewed. The PA representatives present oral reports of their ministries (plus written summaries), an assessment is made of the needs of the church in the region, the needs of the ministries, and the opportunities. Finally, the priority joint activities of the partnership are agreed upon for the coming year. In the PA reports, the presenters highlight their ministries' main activities in the previous year, the objectives for the current year, and an overview of significant trends in the region and in their ministries.

— held annually

— all Partner Agencies invited

— partnership activities reviewed

— Partner Agencies representatives give reports of their ministries:

    — highlight main activities

    — objectives for the current year

    — overview of significant trends in the region and in ministry

— partnership evaluation and assessment:

    — church in the region

    — ministries

    — opportunities

— partnership agrees priority joint activities for the current year

Joint Activities Undertaken by the SEP

The following are the joint activities which have been undertaken or are presently being undertaken by the SEP. Where possible, they have been listed in chronological order:

1. **Follow Up**: the PA acknowledged that there was often inefficient and sometimes dangerous duplication of in-country follow-up visits to media contacts. The media agencies were also aware that they were not effectively following up the many Bible correspondence course students who were completing their courses.

The result was the coordination of follow-up visits, the sharing of information, the coordination of ongoing follow-up procedures in the region, and the training of visitors and OTG discipling personnel.

One colleague from within one of the countries writes in his prayer-letter:

"One focus this year has been on the evangelism and discipleship of Bible correspondence course students. Two faithful men have emerged as well as a fair number of whom we are calling, 'seekers,' serious inquirers struggling with the teachings of the Bible versus their own religious book."

2. **Literature Development**: the most significant thing that came out of a SEP Literature Consultation was the desire to encourage and enable national Christians to write programs for national Christians. David C. Cook staff and Donald Banks acted as consultants. The working group drew up a list of pertinent regional issues which needed addressing; e.g., the occult and marriage. The group also identified the need for a facilitating editor—a national Christian with the experience, gifts, skills, and acceptability to the national Christians to come alongside potential writers and work with them on projects. An ideal candidate made a successful pilot visit, but he was not able to take up the appointment.

The other main decision of the group was to encourage the production of a magazine for second generation nationals living in Europe. After a long gestation period 1,000 copies of such a magazine are soon to be printed.

Another meeting was held the week before the consultation and identified the following areas:

  - cooperative print ventures
  - the avoidance of duplicating publications
  - the necessity of good market research and product
    evaluation.

3. **Cassette Development:** Viggo Sogaard led a PA Cassette Consultation. The participating agencies caught a vision for the role of audio cassettes in evangelism. However, the results so far have been disappointing. The main problem within the SEP has been a lack of personnel with the vision and the ability to realize the potential of this medium.

4. **Bible Correspondence Course Ministries:** a writers' workshop was held and the participants benefitted from the cross-fertilization of ideas. One long-term result of this consultation has been that the three main Bible correspondence course centers represented in the partnership share their course materials and jointly seek to develop new courses.

5. **Signal Strength Research:** the results of a jointly sponsored signal strength field research project are still being analyzed by the media agencies, but the findings will be important for future radio development in the region.

6. **Joint Radio Production:** at the R/PM in January 1989 the idea of joint radio program production was first proposed. The media agencies met in the fall of that year to discuss the implications of joint production and to agree on guidelines. In the spring of 1990 twelve pilot programs were made by four agencies in a training and production period of two weeks.

As a result of the experience it was decided to launch a joint program in the fall of 1990. Three media PA are now participating in this project and producing six 30-minute programs per week. This represents 57 percent of that language broadcast to the region on the PA station. In addition, careful bridging to the succeeding program results in that percentage rising to 80. This joint program replaced two blocks of independent programming being produced by two of the agencies.

7. **Dialectal Radio Project:** as a result of discussions in the fall of 1989 which were taking place alongside the joint program planning, it was decided that it was appropriate and necessary to enlarge an existing regional dialectal radio block. The most significant development has been the partnership between a national agency and several expatriate agencies which brings together the language producers and

follow-up personnel, the funding agency (also providing the core program material), the broadcaster, and no less than three other support agencies.

8. **National Church/Expatriate Agency Relations**: this has been the most difficult area as there has been suspicion on both sides about the nature of the SEP. An in-region meeting was held and this has helped to improve relationships, to rectify misunderstandings, and to encourage closer consultation. There is still much to do in this area.

9. **Other Joint Projects**: geographic response analysis, mailing, and joint fund raising.

Independent Parallel Partnership Activities

Outside the formal SEP activities, there have also been other ongoing partnership activities. The most effective has been a short-term summer Bible school program which has taken place every summer for the last five years. For two weeks in August recommended national Christians have come together for serious biblical study.

Three PA are cooperating in this venture and the teaching has now almost entirely been handed over to trained and able national Christians. The success of this independent joint project and the desire to avoid duplication with other training activities brought short-term pastoral and theological education onto the R/PM agenda for 1991.

Financial Participation in the Partnership

Working together costs something. Not only do the senior representatives of the PA have to budget for the annual R/PM but they also have to make provision for the different consultations which they or members of their teams will be attending. In addition, there is the contribution the PA make to Interdev's budget as a facilitating agency. Neither expense is excessive. One PA has to budget an amount of $10,000 for consultation activities and $2,000 as a voluntary contribution to Interdev (this amounts to 3.25 percent of their annual operational expenditure).

The procedure for contributing to Interdev's facilitating role is still evolving. Originally, Interdev raised 80 percent of the budget they fixed for the SEP initiative. The other 20 percent was provided by the PA. The procedure SEP had adopted prior to January 1990 to meet the amount was through a secret "ballot," each PA pledging itself to a certain sum.

However, a Steering Committee was appointed in January 1990 and new guidelines and a new procedure are being implemented (see Supplement: Draft Steering Committee Proposal). The proposed voluntary contributions are based on the size, resources, and the degree of participation of each PA. Interdev now presents to the PA the annual budgeted operational cost to facilitate the SEP. This excludes staff salaries. In 1991 this figure is $30,632 and the PA are seeking to provide 50 percent of this amount.

Evaluation

Strengths:

1) Working together in unity is a fundamental biblical principle because it expresses the love of Christ in common body life. This is particularly important against the background of the dominant religion in the area.

2) Interdev acts as an independent facilitator/catalyst for the various mission agencies. This independence insures that the agenda is never dominated by any one agency. The small agencies have the same voice as the big ones. In addition, Interdev also functions as an international networker to provide professional Christian trainers for the special interest groups; e.g., ex-British Broadcasting Corporation staff for the radio track, David C. Cook Foundation for literature.

3) The R/PM effectively identifies the common priorities of the PA. The year's partnership agenda does not negate the separate and particular agendas of each agency. Interdev facilitates the PA to write their own common agenda and then to answer for themselves their own questions and problems.

4) The annual oral and written reports of the PA insure that projects are not duplicated and permit synthesis, convergence, and creative cross-fertilization of ideas. In addition, Interdev circulates clear and thorough reports of all the meetings which maintain the focus of the commonly agreed projects.

5) Training together in the specialist groups reduces costs and enriches the experience.

6) Planning together avoids the duplication of ministries and the unnecessary duplication of resources which could otherwise be both time consuming and economically wasteful.

7) Sharing common burdens in Christian fellowship brings encouragement and a sense of accountability and responsibility.

8) There is strength in an inclusive partnership of like-minded missionary and national agencies which represent a wide variety of ministries. This fosters a vertical integration of ministries so maximizing each agency's distinct potential for the Kingdom.

9) A synergism is generated by the partnership. This is the result of the cooperative action between the agencies whose combined effect is greater than the sum of their separate effects.

10) Partnership builds mutual respect and trust between agencies.

Weaknesses:

1) Accountability: there is no one "director." Each agency takes upon itself certain commitments. If it does not keep them, then that particular project suffers. Any joint project is as strong as its weakest link.

2) Tensions between agencies: these are normally creative but the "bigger" members can be tempted to control the agenda while the smaller agencies can become too dependent upon the larger.

3) Slow: a project moves at the speed of the slowest member of the partnership involved. This is being overcome by the recognition, in certain instances, of project leaders. However, it is generally correct to say that only where an Interdev team member or a PA leader is actively involved in being a go-between and a facilitator does a project really progress. The danger for Interdev is that it then becomes a PA and not an external catalyst. The catalyst image breaks down because Interdev changes its nature. An active PA leader can also be detracted from his full-time responsibilities and incur additional expenses for his agency's budget.

4) Lack of tangible results in some areas: it is hard in the short-term to evaluate long-term joint media projects. A lot of the positive results of the Interdev process are the results of working together and simply meeting together to discuss common issues, be they broad overviews or specialist areas. The quality of growing personal relationships is hard to quantify.

5) Language: the present language of the R/PM is almost 100 percent English. To involve more national Christians in the process, there needs to be a greater use of the national and second language in the meetings. This is beginning to happen. The working groups are better and at least one of the groups executes its business 100 percent in the second language with minutes of meetings available in that language as well as in English.

6) Security: some have feared that the reports of the R/PM which are confidential are still too detailed and accessible. Reference to the SEP in more publicly accessible literature is very general.

7) Lack of participation by national Christians: this is a constant source of frustration for a number of the PA. However, it is sometimes hard to find official "representatives" of the national church in a context where there are very few church fellowships.

8) The economic disparity of the agencies has sometimes resulted in the inability of a PA to attend the R/PM. This is particularly true of the national mission agencies and the Two-Thirds world agencies.

9) Other obstacles: At a recent convention in another region of the same language group, the following statement was published under the title, "Obstacles that have hindered cooperation in the past." They included:

- the traditional concepts that have dominated the region for the last 150 years
- the theological differences
- the Western versus the regional standards in such matters as cultural problems
- political overtones

Next Steps

Future agendas of the SEP will have to address the issues raised under the subtitle "Weaknesses." Long-term projects which are being discussed include biblical and pastoral discipleship and training, increased national input at the OTG and media levels, research, recruiting media-related personnel, video development, and media training. Finally, in consultation with the PA, the Steering Committee will have to define its role more clearly and ensure that it clearly communicates this to the SEP.

Conclusion

In conclusion, this short presentation has demonstrated what can be achieved for the Kingdom when national and expatriate agencies seek to work together in a Regional Partnership with a common objective. The region is closed to traditional missionary methods, and there are few national Christian fellowships. In this spiritual and physically hostile environment, Regional Partnership is essential if the

Great Commission is to be accomplished. There must be:
- a **conviction** that partnership is based on Biblical authority
- a **commitment** to evangelism and church planting before self-interest and denominationalism
- a **sacrifice** of exclusive short-term secondary objectives to mutually inclusive long-term priority goals

Supplement

Draft Steering Committee Guidelines

1. Definition of the Strategic Evangelism Partnership

The Strategic Evangelism Partnership, hereafter to be indicated by the abbreviation SEP, is a voluntary body of national church representatives, national agencies, and foreign missions. These groups have agreed to work together in unity to further the Kingdom of God in the region.

The Partnership is facilitated by Interdev through their staff. They have appointed one full-time coordinator to the SEP.

2. The composition of the Steering Committee and its (s)election

A Steering Committee shall be (s)elected by the full Partnership at their annual Review and Planning Meeting. The Committee shall have four members and they shall reflect the nature of the ministries participating in the Partnership.

Each Partner Agency shall have one vote (voice) unless they have more than one distinct ministry. Those agencies shall be allowed two votes, if they so desire.

The Interdev SEP Coordinator shall be ex-officio.

The Committee shall appoint from among themselves a Chairman and a Secretary.

Each member shall serve for a maximum of three years. At least one year shall intervene before a member can be re-(s)elected to the Committee.

3. Responsibilities of the Steering Committee

The Steering Committee shall:

3.1 Provide advice and counsel and be a reference point for the Interdev Partnership coordinator regarding any matter related to the Partnership.

3.2 Make recommendations to the Partnership on:

3.2.1 Working procedures

3.2.2 Ministry priorities

3.2.3 SEP budget which represents the separate agencies' financial commitment to the coordination of the Partnership. The size of the budget and its apportionment to the Partner Agencies shall be prepared in close consultation with Interdev and the Partner Agencies. It is understood that any recommended partition is an invitation to contribute to the coordination of the Partnership and payment is not obligatory.

3.3 Present reports and make recommendations to Interdev on:

3.3.1 Working relationships between the Partnership and Interdev

3.3.2 Evaluation of the operations and process of the Partnership

3.3.3 Progress, development, and implementation of the agreed cooperative priorities.

3.4 Keep Minutes of its meetings and make these available in a file to the Partnership Agencies at the time of the Annual Review and Planning Meeting.

3.5 Present a written report of its activities during the year to the Partnership Agencies at the time of the Annual Review and Planning Meeting.

Authority

The Steering Committee is advisory in nature and makes recommendations to the Partnership and to Interdev. Interdev will continue to provide direct supervision of its coordinator serving the Partnership.

Frequency of meetings

The Steering Committee will meet at the time of the annual Review and Planning Meeting and at least one other time during the year.

CHAPTER 5

Integrated Groups Report

Facilitator: David Garrison

Abstract: *This working group discussed the context for partnerships and presents five main types of vertical partnerships — all with the goal of encouraging the planting of viable, reproducing churches in unreached groups inside the ten-forty window.*

Goal

"The overarching goal of this working group was to see viable, reproducing, holistic churches planted in unreached populations within the ten-forty window, world A."

Integrated partnerships include diverse ministries that come together for a common cause in a partnership. Inside that dimension, the ultimate goal for our consideration was how to reach the unreached in the ten-forty window. Findings may apply elsewhere, but first we want to see if they will work in the most intractable situations. The aim is to evangelize unreached peoples to the point where they have sufficient understanding of who Jesus is to be able to respond, and then to plant churches there.

Vertical Partnerships Affirmed

The group affirmed the effectiveness of vertical partnerships. Vertical partnerships occur when various Christian agencies enter into a voluntary, integrated, complementary strategy.

1) The **strategic** value

The synergy created by vertical partnerships is uniquely endowed to impact stagnant, hostile unreached environments for the sake of the Gospel.

2) The spiritual value

We recognize that there is a special blessing and powerful witness in working out and making visible our biblical unity as diverse members of the Body of Christ.

Models

Five main types of vertical partnerships were examined.

1. Kaleidoscopic partnership—basic acceptance. This is the least concretized form of partnership. It occurs when diverse and seemingly unrelated ministries are viewed from a single perspective to be working together, though independently, to form a beautiful pattern of evangelization. This term was coined by David Barrett in referring to God's perspective on what is happening. We may be working independently, as separate pieces of broken glass, but viewed from the divine perspective, it flows into a beautiful pattern.

For instance, a situation may take place with an unreached people in which perhaps a single individual, maybe a non-residential missionary, assesses the situation and determines there needs to be Bible translation, tentmakers, and radio broadcasting. But because of certain dynamics within the situation, that agent does not go to the point of trying to deal with a round-table consensus or a constitution. He may network with ten different agencies and individuals, talking to each one of them about what they can do to help bring these people to Jesus Christ. This is still a vertical partnership because there is one person weaving about through the whole situation saying, "Here's how you can contribute to the needs of these people."

2. Awareness-respect model—This model involves an awareness of what is happening but also a mutual respect. It occurs when there is a knowledge of and respect between the various agencies engaged in trying to reach the population. They are not necessarily working together, but they respect one another. They are not at cross purposes, and they are complementary to a certain extent.

3. Consultative partnerships—This is a deeper, more concretized level where members actively seek consultation with each other. This level occurs when the various agencies consult with one another for purposes of achieving an ultimate goal. It may be nothing more than simply informing another person of what one is trying to do in a certain area, or asking, "If I do this, what impact will that make?"

4. Consensus partnerships — These occur when the various agencies go beyond consultation and actually agree to work together to achieve their common goal or goals. This is a desirable situation which can maximize breaking through to an unreached people.

5. Constitutional partnership — This is a yet deeper level and occurs when agencies enter into a formal contractual relationship. Some models would be the International Afghan Mission and the United Mission to Nepal. For instance, to join IAM's mission effort in Khabul, one would need to subscribe to their constitution.

These may be viewed as developmental stages toward more structured partnerships. One of these models may be most appropriate for a particular context. In some contexts where a consensus may never be achieved, an awareness or a kaleidoscopic level may still be reached.

Important Components in Effective Partnership

1. Vision — There must be at least one individual who has a vision for integrated partnership who will share that vision with the various participating agencies.

2. Structure — Some kind of structure is necessary to bring about an integrated partnership.

3. Attitudes — Probably there are more items under attitudes than under any other component. Some of these attitudes are listed in the next section.

4. Commitment — This is more than just an idea. It actually involves dated goals and objectives with a budget, plans for evaluation, and so forth.

5. Relationships — A whole range of components are involved in relationships with equality and mutual respect being major factors. These components are discussed throughout this volume.

6. Expectations — These must be clearly defined. What do we want to see come out of this integrated partnership? Is it a massive thing such as evangelizing an entire people so that they all come to know Jesus Christ, or is it a rather limited thing, such as producing half-hour radio programs on a monthly basis by 1992? Expectations need to be clearly defined.

Characteristics of Healthy Partnerships

accountability

acceptance (of new agencies and denominations—western and indigenous—as well as of cultural preferences)

biblical basis

clear expectations

commitment (to individuals as well as agencies)

common vision

competent facilitators

conflict resolution/reconciliation

demonstrable servanthood

dependability

forgiveness

flexibility/openness to change

honesty

love

maturity (spiritual and relational)

mutual respect

ownership

patience

prayer

presence (allow enough time to listen)

results (must see progress over time in both program and relationships)

sacrifice

sense of humor

sensitive to security needs of all partners

shared success and failure

strong self-identity, along with sensitivity to disparate constituencies

transparency

trust

understanding of need for cross-cultural training

worship together

Resolution

"Celebrating God's use of diverse, individual strategies in the past, in a fresh spirit of cooperation we recommend the development of strategic vertical partnerships aimed at unreached and historically intractable populations across the least-evangelized world."

Section 3

❖❖❖

Church-to-Church Partnerships

CHAPTER 6

The Local Church as a Catalyst

James Moats

Abstract: *Practical considerations for successful church-to-church partnerships between Western and Two-Thirds world churches are discussed by the head of ISSACHAR, an organization that assists local churches in developing a focus on unreached people groups.*

Introduction

Perhaps you've not thought about it. Just what is required to complete the task of world evangelization? If someone asked you to name the three resources most needed, which items would you emphasize? Where would these resources come from? At Issachar, we have been thinking about this.

In 1986 Issachar was invited by the Lausanne Committee for World Evangelization to lead Project Jericho. A massive undertaking, Project Jericho was designed to link Christian leaders from forty restricted nations to the worldwide evangelical movement. At the 1989 Lausanne Congress in Manila, 500 men and women from these nations came together to worship, fellowship, study, and strategize to reach their nations for Christ.

During this project, it became clear that the church is capable of completing the Great Commission and that it has adequate resources. This project also proved that distribution is the primary problem. Lausanne Committee statistics show 12,000 unreached people groups and 416 Christian churches per unreached people group.

As we reflected on the nature and flow of the critical resources from the evangelized world to the unreached world, we recognized two important principles:

1) There are only three critical resources involved in world evangelization: people, money, and prayer.

2) All of these resources flow from the local church.

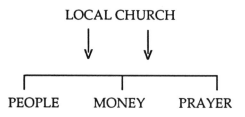

LOCAL CHURCH

PEOPLE   MONEY   PRAYER

Since 1974 much work has been done through the U. S. Center for World Mission and other organizations to create a broad-based, conceptual understanding of dividing the unevangelized world linguistically rather than geo-politically. Much of that work has remained conceptual and has not transitioned onto the field.

In response to this need, Issachar has begun assisting local churches in developing a focus on unreached people groups. Church-to-church partnerships are simply one strategy for accomplishing this. Our desire is to link North American local churches with local churches that are located geographically near a specific unreached people group.

The History of Church-to-Church Partnerships

Our research showed that church-to-church partnerships have been tried and tested over many years with varying levels of success. Out of this experience, some key principles have emerged.

1) Those churches that had become deeply involved with church partnerships had experienced significant change. The key element was **deep exposure**. Those that had superficial exposure, equivalent to sending financial support or becoming pen pals, experienced almost no change. Deep exposure meant that a significant number of members from one church, including the senior pastor, travelled to the partner church and vice versa.

2) We learned that there were no examples of church-to-church partnerships effectively evangelizing an unreached people group. However, we believed that this was an issue of intentionality and that by intentionally targeting an unreached people group this point could be overcome.

Lessons Learned

We learned several important lessons along the way that caused us to modify our approach away from church-to-church partnerships.

There must be a commitment to the unreached. People in churches give their hearts away to charismatic leaders without considering the consequences. Where partnerships were started without first developing a vision for an unreached people group, the purpose of the partnership became a relationship. While this has merit, we have found great difficulty in trying to elevate this partnership to a higher level, that of reaching the unreached people group. Since our goal for this project was to reach unreached people groups, this early lesson caused us to wonder if this model would be successful.

The senior pastor must take the lead. We recognized the importance of the senior pastor's commitment to the project. To penetrate an unreached people requires an intensive, long-term commitment. This commitment cannot be maintained unless the senior pastor and the other leaders of the church have given their hearts away to the unreached people group.

Vision cannot be transferred. It must be birthed. The North American church has historically used stories and a variety of visual aids to stimulate vision in the church. This form of stimulation does not build vision. It simply arouses interest and expectations that cannot be fulfilled without field exposure. Therefore an experience-based pathway needs to be created by the church through which vision can be birthed. Once vision is birthed in the hearts of some members through short-term field exposure, then each of these people can influence ten more to seek out a similar learning experience. Missions committees need to incorporate short-term trips as part of their effort to facilitate vision in the local church.

Stories build expectations. As an increasing number from the church live among the unreached for short periods of time, they bring back their own unique stories to the congregation. Each story serves to build upon the past stories, thereby providing a single thread that can run through the entire church, changing missions awareness dramatically. When a church decides to focus on an unreached people group instead of a church partnership, the vision becomes compelling for all partners. This creates a positive culture that sustains a long-term commitment to the process.

Missions is for everyone, not a select few. When a local church departmentalizes missions, it sends out the message that missions is only for a select group. To reach an unreached people group requires that a broad, cross-section of people of all ages, education, work experience, and economic levels be exposed to the unreached people group. This requires careful planning so that the traditional mission committee ownership trap can be avoided. Ownership for this project should be broadened immediately beyond the missions committee. Our experience indicates that leadership for the project will develop when the senior pastor recruits select leaders from the church to travel with him to the unreached people. The selection of this initial team will serve as the launching pad for church mobilization. We recommend that the composition of the team be carefully and prayerfully considered.

Missions must serve as a resource for all departments. If this project is perceived as a missions committee project, then other church departments may view it competitively. To avoid this, the missions committee needs to be established at the church level (instead of the customary missions committee level) and should serve as a resource center for interested parties.

Resource the project through a business and professional fellowship. Most of the people in the church are detached from active missions, which automatically means that prayer and money are of limited supply. Further, most mission-minded churches are fully committed with their present funding and people. Reaching an unreached people group will require that this network be substantially broadened into the business and professional segment of the congregation. Our experience indicates that these people are problem solvers and will commit their time and money once they believe in the project. For this reason we recommend that a business and professional fellowship be established to resource this project with the missions committee serving their needs as the project develops.

The local church must develop a better understanding of the field. By itself, a church does not have the ability to reach the unreached people group without first becoming a mission agency. A new division of responsibility is needed between the church and the agency. Since the local church is the source of all people, money, and prayer, it must provide visionary leadership for the project. Mission agencies should be viewed as service agencies providing the administrative and support systems necessary to deliver specific field expertise. It is important that the North American church develop its vision for the unreached people group and then an understanding of the field. This will pave the way for a more functional relationship with the field agencies as well as empowering the church to serve as a catalyst.

The local church must develop a better understanding of the tools available to reach a people group. When a local church understands all the possibilities that could be used to effectively evangelize a people group, it is able to more wisely invest its people, money, and prayer and make a more intentional selection of field agency assistance. Churches must move from the casual to the intentional if success is to result.

Churches that commit substantial resources to one or two unreached people groups can serve as a catalyst. The North American church is captive to its culture. It has developed a project mentality that feeds on quick results and has no infrastructure for sustaining a focused, long-term commitment to evangelizing a people group. Therefore, the church should work with an intermediary who is willing to coach it through the process of developing that infrastructure. Evidence indicates that once infrastructure and culture are developed, the possibilities for field impact are endless.

Most mission service agencies can maximize the resources of the local church to effectively evangelize an unreached people group. The church often lacks the necessary resources to carry out an effective missions enterprise. Churches who are able to make a substantial resource commitment to one or two unreached people groups will serve as catalyst. Their resources and vision can draw together a select group of service agencies who then become integrated to reach the people group.

Resource agencies need to package information in a way that is meaningful to the local church. During the past decade, dozens of resource agencies in North America have developed information to assist the missions enterprise. Unfortunately, no one has packaged this information in ways that are meaningful to the local church. Issachar is committed to presenting this material in a language and context that is understandable to the local church in order to encourage a stronger local church resource participation that will transform the missions enterprise.

Informed churches can change the agencies' views of the value of the local church in the missions frontier. Interviews with mission agency leaders indicate that they are generally cynical of the local church. Most believe that the local church desires to be entertained, instead of accomplishing something substantial. Therefore, many agency/church relationships remain typically shallow and almost never transcend to the more difficult issues that require creative solutions. Changing this will ultimately bring about an army of Christians toward the unreached. Informed churches can change the agency's view of the local church and at the same time provide the accountability that all agencies need. Both of these are lacking in the missions enterprise and must become an urgent matter for change.

Emerging Model

Once we understand and apply these principles we see the local church emerging as a catalyst through the informed investment of its strategic resources to evangelize unreached peoples.

Figure 6.1 uses the Uzbeks of Soviet Central Asia to illustrate this point. Each bar on the chart represents one mission tool; from missionaries on the ground, to radio broadcasting, to television, to literature, all the way through the complete list of ministry possibilities. This is a partial list, and the possibilities will be limited only by the assets and creativity of the local church and its partners. Additionally, each of these bars usually represents a mission agency which has historically developed along specialized lines. It is the job of the catalyst to bring together multiple specialists to carry out the desired task. People, money, and prayer can develop this cohesive relationship between the local church and the mission agencies, especially when several local churches combine to form a consortium aimed at a particular unreached people group.

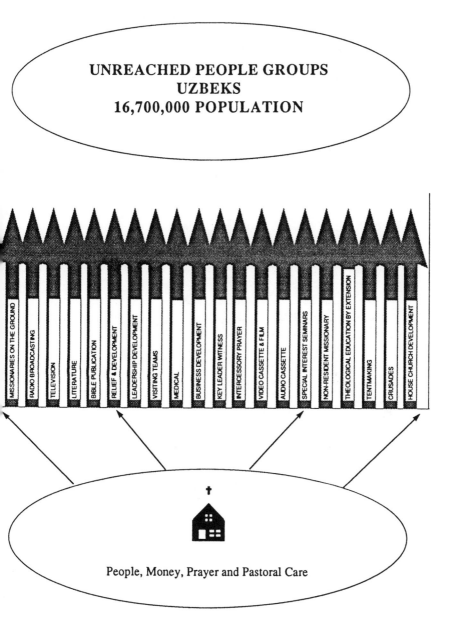

Figure 6.1

Figure 6.2 shows the Enosis (contemporary Greek meaning "to link or unite") model where the North American Church serves as catalyst, and vision is formed as it views its relationship with the unreached people group. This vision is fulfilled when its strategic resources (people, money, and prayer) are allocated through its own efforts and those of the mission agencies.

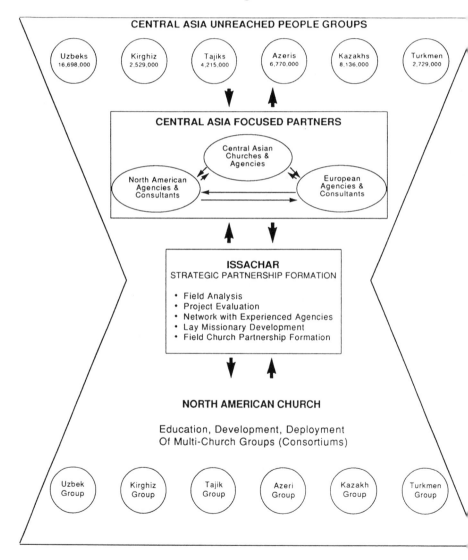

Figure 6.2

Emerging Principles

As the Enosis Concept continues to develop, several principles are becoming apparent.

Selection Principle

The most important principle is one of selection. Churches must select agencies and partners who have the same vision. Time must be given to developing trust in a manner where all parties benefit from the relationship. Since some of the agencies will be located overseas, an intermediary could help provide some of the legwork to see that the relationships develop at a healthy pace. Issachar has chosen to fulfill this role. Eventually these relationships could become a strong bridge capable of sustaining much traffic as increased resources are funnelled through field service agencies and the local church to reach the unreached people group.

Priority Principle

The larger the church the more capacity it has to initiate multiple new projects. However, regardless of size, this project will probably be most churches' largest mission project and should be treated accordingly. If it is not treated in this fashion, intra-church competition will diminish its chances for success.

Planning Principle

As the church increases in influence and moves into a catalystic role, it must develop a very strong sense of stewardship of its God-given resources. To do this, it needs to develop a firsthand understanding of the unreached people group. It should have a fairly adequate assessment of the plans presently underway as well as those for the future. This will assist the church in deciding on the most appropriate way to allocate scarce resources. *The principle of planning is most important in this model and therefore requires each church to experience several months of research and learning, before moving into action.*

This may be a difficult lesson for many churches, but one that will pay big dividends both for the unreached, as well as retraining the church in wise stewardship.

CHAPTER 7

Church-to-Church Partnership
What? Why? How?

James Glynn

Abstract: *This presentation details the five-fold nature of church-to-church relationships. It presents these partnerships as the kind that will produce in greatest quantity and quality members of God's church around the world as well as encouraging the greatest participation by individual members of the Body in fulfilling the Great Commission. A case study of the Cross and Crown Church partnership with Jonc D'Odin Church in Haiti is given.*

Introduction

God intended the members of his church to take care of each another, to stand in Christ's place and support, encourage, stimulate, inspire, and empower one another. "Therefore, as we have opportunity, let us do good to all people, especially to those who belong to the family of believers" (Gal. 6:10 NIV).

It is so easy when talking about the subject of partnership to confine our conversation and most of our strategies to every type of partnership *except* the kind that will produce in largest numbers and greatest depth the units of God's people around the world as well as the individual participation of the members of the body of Christ in fulfilling the Great Commission. When local churches partner with one another cross-culturally, the Lord does something unique. Each partner is enriched and empowered beyond the limits of their previous capabilities, and that empowering then becomes the cornerstone of the Great Commission harvests in both fields.

What is Church-to-Church Partnership?

It is a *relationship* fivefold in nature. First, it is *reciprocal*. Two local churches come together as partners across normal cultural barriers for mutual benefit. Our spiritual and physical needs are matched as we each realize what can be given and what can be received. Hospitality, love, prayer, healing, knowledge, material gifts, example, leadership, hope, friendship—these are but a few. We realize from the beginning that the value of our exchange will be equal in everyone's eyes and of mutual benefit for immediate, long-range, and eternal purposes.

Second, the relationship is *intimate*. Barriers are broken down. We see, feel, and embrace the needs of fellow members of Christ's body. We come to know and love one another in depth as we search out felt needs instead of assumed needs. We pray, listen, and plan our solutions together with one another before the Lord.

Third, the relationship is *ongoing*. Continuity, maturity, and growth are essential as the Lord leads us in partnership with people who, apart from our oneness in faith, seem so different. We need to make the kind of commitment to one another involving enough time to make many mistakes and then to grow to a deep understanding, maturity, and fruitfulness in fulfilling the plans of heaven.

Fourth, the relationship is *practical*. We come together to equip one another in our areas of strength and to sit at one another's feet in our areas of weakness. We challenge one another to fulfill the Great Commission of Christ and we enable one another to more straightly walk the narrow path. With wise, informed giving, the partner richer in the goods of this world participates in self-help and cooperative projects, and with wisdom from above, the partner rich in the things of eternity lays out its life in prayer, spiritual discipline, faith, and hope.

Finally, the relationship is *spiritual*, aimed at the spiritual enrichment of all involved, and ultimately, at the further task of facing the harvesting fields of the world hand in hand, demonstrating the kind of unity that Jesus was talking about when he said, "...there shall be one flock and one shepherd" (John 10:16 NIV) and "...that all of them may be one, Father, just as you are in me and I am in you ... so that the world may believe..." (John 17:21 NIV).

Why Should We Have Church-to-Church Partnerships?

First, because it is a work *begun in God's heart*. In Ephesians 3:1-10, we are told about the most profound mystery, the awesome wonder of God founding a new entity on earth—the Church of Jesus Christ, a body in which people of different cultures, races, and languages are unified together with the Lord. Note also the following Scriptures in the light of this discussion: Ephesians 2:11-19 and 2 Corinthians 8:1-6.

Second, because the *need is great!* We so easily get overwhelmed and then paralyzed by massive need. We believe Satan's lie, "Small attempts to help accomplish nothing." If church planting efforts worldwide were both preceded and followed by warm hands of love and encouragement from a cross-cultural partner, how might its results multiply? Not only is the need great, though, in the sense we would normally think, but Western Christians also need desperately to experience the living faith, love, and sacrifice of Two-Thirds world Christians. We need the injection of spiritual vitality from their witness to us, which pales anything physical or material we might offer them.

Third, the *time has come.* God is doing something new in the world, perhaps in preparation for his coming again, perhaps in the world-wide awakening and revival to hasten world evangelization. The world is more and more becoming a global village. Personal involvement in missions for so many Westerners is easily within the realm of possibility. Moreover, this generation of Christians more than ever before is sensing a responsibility for hands-on, high-touch, relational ministry in every area of Christ's call.

There is yet another reason that could be seen as crucial in understanding why now is the time to form partnerships. I recently read an article which spoke of the ramifications of the United States taking a lowered position among world cultures. We may remain rich materially but we may not remain the nation with every other desirable egg in our cultural basket.

The mightiest signs of God's present visitation and the corresponding results in breadth of church growth and depth of discipleship is already in the Two-Thirds world. In the kingdom of God, we are truly seeing the eleventh-hour workers receiving the same pay as those who have been laboring in the fields all day. We are seeing the spiritual child become more intimate in the Word and prayer and witness than the spiritual parent. We are seeing national Christians growing so quickly in spirit that they soon "overshadow" in discernment, commitment, spiritual gifts, and discipline the very missionaries who first brought them the Gospel. It is time for the "teachers" to trade places, in many instances, with the students.

With this in mind, how clear it is that we in the West are perhaps the most in need of partnership with the churches in countries where the Gospel is setting lives on fire, and where it is happening in closer proximity to unreached people groups.

How Do We Form Church-to-Church Partnerships?

Simply put, partnerships between local churches will operate best for most situations when carried out with a board or agency to act as guide, aid, planner, translator, and coordinator in this kind of hands-on involvement.

The most critical, ongoing link needs to be a cross-cultural staff, usually composed of both Western missionaries and national Christian leaders, who:

- chooses the "sister" church
- trains the national church while the Western church is also in training and preparation
- acts as liaison between the churches
- meets visiting groups and arranges translation, transportation, meals, and lodging
- aids the national church in planning lodging, meals, work projects, and other preparations for a visiting team
- translates songs, letters, and other correspondence on an ongoing basis between the two churches
- plans future projects and ministries with the churches
- supervises all community development projects from beginning to end, long after the Western team has returned home
- provides tools, generators, sound systems, musical instruments, and other items for visiting teams

What are the Benefits of Church-to-Church Partnership?

Here is one place where the entire church body can become involved in communication, preparation, sponsorship, or hands-on participation. Through this kind of partnering, world missions becomes personalized.

We better understand the ups and downs of missionaries and nationals and are better able to minister to them. We gain insight into real problems and complicated solutions facing the Two-Thirds world; we will never again fall into the folly of simplistic answers because we have seen for ourselves. We will spend more time in prayer realizing that we may be rich but not very wise. Church-to-church partnership most often releases awakening and revival into a church, releasing people for witness at home and abroad. Young people and old people are moved to give their lives to Christian service and to recognize the worth of their unique spiritual gifts as never before.

Most important, as in a marriage, when our lives are committed "till death do us part" with someone so different from us, we discover that the Lord had a purpose which began with a miracle called *unity*, but which did not end there. He brings us together for a purpose no less universal than the evangelization of the world.

Problems That Must Be Addressed in Church-to-Church Partnership

1) When individual congregations partner with one another cross-culturally, it opens up all ongoing problems with the missionaries who currently or previously have worked in the area. Many of the missionaries see the Western church as "intruders" and are not convinced that any good can come from the partnering.

National leaders and church members can contribute to this problem by heaping praise upon the partner church, especially in areas which are weaknesses of the missionaries. On the one hand, this can force the visiting partner team to refrain from all judgments and to do their best to understand the role of the missionaries with their normal assets and liabilities. On the other hand, it can cause the missionaries to "recapture their first love" and themselves receive the inspiration and ministry offered by the visiting team.

In this same regard, it is vital that the enabling agency does not regard the partnership ministry as a poor stepchild of the "real" world missions task. Everyone from agency executives to missionaries need to catch a vision of the best possibilities to be realized in long-term church-to-church partnership.

2) There are also problems in the lack of cross-cultural sensitivities among the visiting team. Expressed acts of love and normal Christian graces will cover many cultural faux pas. However, it is helpful when the visiting teams receive orientation to the host culture and church and when some preparation in cross-cultural communication and basic language is given.

However, instead of concentrating on the difficulties, since this side of heaven there will *always* be problems, it is possible to walk right through them and carry on a glorious partnership. It is worth all the continuously unresolved issues. It's worth the stigma that can get attached to the visiting team when one or two come to the field as "ugly Americans" or attempt to buy fast solutions to cross-cultural problems. All members must concentrate on the best that the Holy Spirit can produce through the relationship. Most of all, they must concentrate on their *unity* in Christ despite any appearances to the contrary.

3) It is so difficult to erase our superiority complex as Westerners. We tend to think of ourselves in the United States as the "senders" just because we may be the "initiators." We may initiate these partner relationships simply because we have the ability to travel and send teams. Our sense of primacy in the partner relationship is based only on our money, not on how the Lord regards us. The humility and then the maturity that results from seeing our true position with one another in partnership follows a long-term relationship of prayer. We can erase everything that creates superior/inferior complexes when we are as ready to receive as we are to give. This is perhaps one of the greatest keys to success in church-to-church partnership.

Case Study

The relationship between Cross and Crown Community Church in Arlington Heights, Illinois, and Jonc D'Odin Church in Haiti began in mid-1982 during a time of evaluation and long-range planning when I, as pastor, realized that we at Cross and Crown had absolutely no awareness or hands-on participation in world missions apart from the offerings sent to the denominational headquarters. I was convicted to pray for some way to motivate our congregation in missions.

About a month later, I was visited by a representative of Worldteam. That agency was in the beginning stages of a new program which they called "Reciprocal Care" in which they were seeking American churches to become sister churches to evangelical congregations in Haiti, the poorest country in our hemisphere. This was designed to be a permanent relationship in which, year after year, we would find ways to mutually share and grow in our oneness and ministry in Christ. It would require deep commitment and a minimum of money. In years to come, as we sent ministry teams, youth groups, pastoral training teams, or construction crews to Haiti, we were assured that what we received in love and spiritual growth would far outweigh anything we might give. Through the relationship and our complementary strengths, we would be equipping each other for more effective witness and outreach.

We started the ministry within a few months of that first visit from Worldteam. We received the name, location, and other information about the church chosen for us—a large rural church of about 500 members in a town called Jonc D'Odin. The pastor, Duphar Alexis, had a family including a wife and six children. We first introduced ourselves by making a big Christmas banner with signatures of our members to send to Haiti. Then we began planning for the first team visit from Cross and Crown. We met three hours weekly for more than three months, learning Haitian history, geography, politics, economics, culture, religion, and as much as possible of the Creole language spoken in Haiti.

Summary

August, 1983. Six members from Cross and Crown formed the first team to Jonc D'Odin. We worshipped three times in the church in addition to singing and preaching in two other churches. We also provided 100 French Bibles which the pastor began giving away, one each week, to the person who brought the most visitors to worship. The first Sunday after we left, one man brought 75 non-Christian members of his village in order to receive the first Bible.

We led a women's retreat for 200, a men's retreat for 100, and a children's retreat for 300, including teaching, singing, crafts, games, and prayer. We also met for a number of hours with the deacons of Jonc D'Odin Church. This became an annual event where we could learn about each other; share both spiritual, personal, and material needs; plan future strategies; and pray for one another. When I became ill, the pastor's wife cared for me as though I were her child, binding our families together in a relationship of love and care that nothing can ever sever. When we returned home, I printed up a journal, showed slides, and played tapes so that all member of Cross and Crown could feel they had been there.

July, 1984. Seven members from Cross and Crown led a couples' retreat at our sister church, an all-day family picnic, a youth rally for 150 teens, an all-day youth leaders' retreat, and visited people family by family in their homes throughout the countryside.

August, 1985. Ten Cross and Crown members formed a work team with the men of Jonc D'Odin Church to construct a Home Economics Center next to the church building. This three-room building became the center of a three-year program in which young women learned crochet, embroidery, sewing, and cooking along with Bible study, singing, and prayer. By this time I was learning to master the Creole language and began to translate songs into their language. We also led a two-morning women's retreat, a two-evening men's retreat, showed a slide program on the life of Christ to a packed church of members and non-Christian neighbors, and even attended a wedding at which I was asked to preach.

May, 1986. Pastor and Mme. Duphar came to visit Cross and Crown Church. We planned special events during their two-week stay, giving them opportunities to minister to our people in a variety of small-group settings. These events included lunch with senior citizens, a reception in our home, an interview on the Moody radio station, and speaking at both an elementary and junior high school.

When they left, one of our members gave a very touching testimony, listing not only what we had given the Duphars, but also what they had freely and lovingly given us—their wisdom, their love for the Lord, their honesty, hope, and courage.

August, 1986. The Associate Pastor and I went to Haiti to lead a youth retreat to equip leaders of all the churches in the Jonc D'Odin District, to visit an evangelistic outstation run by the deacons of our sister church, and to discuss self-help and cooperative projects with the national church leader in charge of community development.

June, 1987. A sad day in this reciprocal program. The morning that nine people were ready to depart for a visit to our sister church, the phone rang and we were told that revolution had broken out and it would be too dangerous for us to come.

March, 1988. With two weeks notice, three of us prepared ourselves for a trip in which we met again with the community development leader, preached a funeral, visited the Home Economics Center and the Jonc D'Odin School in action, and visited deacons one by one in their homes, witnessing and participating in daily spiritual disciplines.

July, 1988. The nine members whose trip was aborted last year regrouped and completed their mission. One Black from a church in Chicago accompanied our team this time—a wonderful addition from the Haitian point of view as they were accustomed to thinking that all North Americans are white and rich. This team, together with brothers and sisters from Jonc D'Odin, painted the entire church and Home Economics Center; held an all-day women's retreat for 300; conducted a half-day children's festival; opened the Community Co-op Store; met with young single adults; and attended a baptism of new members in a nearby river.

August, 1989. Fourteen Cross and Crown members on a "Musical Ministry Tour" shared both Creole and English songs in concerts in many different churches. This team had a powerful evangelistic outreach, ministering to churches overflowing with non-Christians. The team also led a retreat for wives of pastors and elders, a district youth retreat, and painted another church in the district.

August, 1989–March, 1990. The 25-year-old son of Pastor Duphar came to the U. S., lived in my home, and attended a school for training in diesel mechanics in order to be able to support himself and launch a ministry in Port-au-Prince.

June, 1990. Five members of Cross and Crown took five deacons and Pastor Duphar on a four-day retreat to Cap Haitien, visiting historic sites that none of them had seen before, and spending time with them in prayer, sharing, planning, and rest. Not one of these servants of the Lord had ever taken a day off. The team built thirty new benches for the school, held an evangelistic service showing the "Jesus" film, and led a retreat for young people.

May, 1991. Pastor Duphar was sent a ticket to come to our First Annual Global Missions Conference and be a keynote speaker at our International Dinner.

July, 1991. Seven members of Cross and Crown were preparing to go to Haiti as Team #9 in July.

Evaluation

It may be helpful to share the following insights:

1) Year-round contact is maintained with the sister church. Letters go back and forth so each Body has a sense of their responsibility to keep the other informed so all will know how to pray.

2) One indispensable ingredient to the current spiritual awakening seems to be the fact that for the past nine years, a group of women has gathered at Jonc D'Odin Church every Friday at 5 a.m. to pray for Cross and Crown Church.

3) Pastor Duphar says, "The greatest gift you have given is not the money or projects or any material thing, though we are extremely grateful for these. But most important, you have given us hope, a reason to persevere, a sign of God's love made tangible in the midst of suffering. You have given us the gift of yourselves..."

4) As the relationship has progressed through the years, it has matured. In the beginning we wanted to collect material things to give to our Haitian brothers and sisters. As the years have continued, however, we are learning more about how to be the most effective in our aid, especially in establishing self-help and cooperative projects.

5) My own personal commitment as pastor has been at the heart of this program. I feel now after nine years that I am truly a part of the Haitian family and they are a part of ours. My eyes have been lifted far beyond the horizons of my comfortable suburban life, and I have a

living sense of oneness with the world's poor and the world's Christians.

6) With a growing understanding of the frontiers of unreached people groups in the world, we are beginning to talk more seriously with Haitians about our roles in equipping one another to reach the unreached.

7) The effect of this program has been so profound that when Cross and Crown finally was ready to launch a full-scale world missions program, at the first World Missions Conference, 100 members pledged nearly $55,000 in faith promises—and this from a church where most people already tithe in their regular offerings.

We concluded every concert of the 1989 musical tour with this song:

> Make us one, Father God, make us one,
> > That the world may know you gave your only Son.
> Fill us with the love you've given us to share,
> > And protect us from the evil everywhere.
> For you have chosen that together we should be
> > A reflection of your love and unity.
> Cleanse us from our old nature of sin,
> > That your image may be seen in us again.
> Send us in the world to be a channel of
> > All the glorious riches of your love.
> And we'll tell the world the truth of how you feel,
> > That the world may know that Jesus' love is real.

CHAPTER 8

Partnerships Involving Elmbrook Church: A Case Study

Val Hayworth

Abstract: *Elmbrook Church has been involved in several unique missions partnerships since 1982. This synopsis does not describe a single relationship, but a history of partnerships focused on unreached people groups. Local churches and facilitating agencies should be motivated toward "possibility planning" and gain insights into the potentialities of close cooperating relationships.*

Introduction

Some hunters like a rifle. They aim carefully, choosing deep penetration in a small area.

Others prefer the shotgun approach. They enthusiastically fire away, scattering shot over a larger area but achieving less impact.

If I may relate this analogy to missions strategy, some missions programs choose to use a rifle. They tightly focus in to make a significant impact on a few small, specific target areas. Others prefer to aim a shotgun somewhere in the general direction of broader targets, trusting that pellets will hit here and there and make some kind of impact.

At Elmbrook, we have chosen more of the rifle approach. Our philosophy behind this decision is the idea that none of us can do everything involved in world evangelization. But some of us can learn to do a few things well as our contribution to that task.

Description of Elmbrook Church

Elmbrook Church is a large suburban fellowship located near Milwaukee. Nearly 5000 regular attenders, college age and older, attend one of the four services each weekend. There are seventeen pastors on the staff including, since 1982, a full-time pastor responsible for the missions ministry. The Senior Pastor, Stuart Briscoe, has traveled extensively in his worldwide ministries and communicates a world concern to the congregation.

Description of the Missions Program

Regular monthly support is provided to 127 missionary units (families or singles) and 13 organizations. Sixty-two of the missionary supportees are members of Elmbrook Church and, in addition, there are five member missionaries who do not require financial support. Support levels range from full support to $110 per month. Typically, a member couple serving overseas is eligible for 60 percent of its support requirement as determined by the mission agency.

Since 1975, the faith promise method for determining the missions' budget has been used. By 1980, the budget was based on a faith promise of $500,000. The first one-million-dollar budget was provided by the fellowship in 1987.

Approximately 45 individuals serve on the Missions Committee, which is divided, for administrative purposes, into a steering committee and five geographical regional groups.

The responsibility for the counseling and mentoring of individuals who express interest in missionary service is primarily that of the Missions Pastor. Elmbrook Church operates a Christian Study Center in conjunction with Trinity Evangelical Divinity School from which students can receive a Certificate of Biblical Studies. Opportunities for the development of ministry skills and cross-cultural sensitivities are abundant.

Background of Partnering Relationships

In 1981-82 the Missions Committee was challenged by its Missionary-In-Residence to concentrate a part of its human and financial resources on an unreached people group, with the goal being the establishment of a reproducing church body. A key component in the strategy was the development of a unique partnership between a mission agency and Elmbrook.

Kenya Target Area and SIM

The Missions Committee was urged to consider the nomadic pastoralists of East Africa. Nearly two years were required to research and select a suitable group, dialogue with potential mission agency partners, and coordinate with indigenous church councils. As the result, a work among the Borana-speaking peoples of north central Kenya was started.

The Missions Committee, with the backing of the fellowship, committed itself to a long term church-planting effort. SIM was selected as the sending agency, and an understanding of cooperation was worked out with the leaders of that organization. By early 1984, two couples were on the field and additional units were preparing for departure midyear. Full support was provided for these missionaries, and annual regular support for the target area project from 1985 was anticipated to be at least $100,000.

The work in Kenya continues in spite of a number of frustrating problems which arose. Major adjustments to the original plan had to be made because of complex jurisdictional matters involving SIM, AIM, and the Africa Inland Church, conflicts about methods of ministry, and strained interpersonal relationships. Despite the problems, the Missions Committee remained convinced that the concept of target area involvements was valid and resolved not to repeat the mistakes of the Kenya effort in other projects.

Caracas Target Area and TEAM

As Elmbrook became more adept and proactive in the recruiting and training of potential missionaries and in carving out its niche in the task of world evangelization, it became obvious that its second target area effort should have a radically different focus than primitive nomadic peoples.

Broad objectives were reaffirmed, but it was determined that the focus should be in an urban environment, that a currently supported missionary with field experience must be available as team leader, and that a carefully worded agreement be worked out with a single compatible agency willing to partner in a unique arrangement with a local church.

Survey work to identify potential cities was initiated. A search committee was formed to identify the partnering agency. Within one year the Holy Spirit had coordinated all aspects of the criteria, and TEAM and Elmbrook had a written agreement in place before team participants were selected. As events unfolded, a Caracas team was formed in which Elmbrook people were a minority, but Elmbrook was the catalyst for the outreach effort.

Target Area Efforts in Conjunction with the Bible League and TransWorld Radio

Elmbrook has attempted to address a few specific shorter term needs in addition to the open-ended commitments described previously. For example, the extraordinary needs of India have been researched and a three-year commitment of financial resources has been made to the Bible League. The objectives include a desire to penetrate a predominantly Hindu area, facilitate the training and ministry of national evangelists, and expedite the distribution of Scriptures. Although a number of fine organizations accomplish one or more of these activities, the Bible League combines all of them in a cost effective package. Elmbrook now has its own Million People Unit target area in the state of Uttar Pradesh.

A second example can be mentioned briefly. Elmbrook has a deep interest in the country of Turkey because of member missionaries who serve there. In 1989-90 the Missions Committee considered ways to enhance the efforts of these supportees, as well as the general evangelization work of the Christian community. The committee discovered that short wave programming was woefully inadequate for the 85-90 million Turks in Europe and Asia. Discussion centered on two options: whether to recruit two more couples for the Turkish field or invest an equivalent annual amount of money in a radio program. For the current year, the clear choice in regard to effective use of resources is radio.

Currently Developing Partnership with a Soviet Church

Early in 1990 the Missions Office dialogued with three agencies promoting sister church relationships in the Soviet Union. One of those organizations, ISSACHAR, had several intriguing ideas about accessing the Muslim republics of Soviet Central Asia and enhancing missions vision and involvement of USA church fellowships. Elmbrook became one of the USA churches qualified to send representatives to the Moscow Congress on Soviet Evangelization last October. A potential sister church was identified in Frunze, Kirghizia, and a visit by four Elmbrook people to Frunze was arranged the week after the Congress.

The purpose of the sister church relationship is not primarily the edification of the two fellowships involved, although this will occur during the minimum five-year commitment the fellowships have made to each other. The ultimate objective is a joint outreach to currently unreached Muslims.

The Missions Committee is dealing with a number of problems. Contact with Central Asian believers is not easily maintained. Communication problems and travel arrangement difficulties abound. A second trip to Frunze has been postponed twice, but four individuals are scheduled to visit in June. There are uncertainties about the needs of specific Soviet churches and few proven strategies for ministry to Soviet Muslim communities. The methods of facilitating agencies are still evolving. The appropriateness of a long-range commitment and specific strategy to the region is still being considered by Elmbrook's Council of Elders.

On the positive side, a surprising number of contacts and opportunities are emerging. The network of individuals and organizations interested in Soviet Central Asia is not insignificant. Business opportunities for bivocational missionaries exist, making a continuous presence possible. Three Elmbrook members have already declared their availability for service. The Missions Committee is tentative about the next steps, but optimistic about what God is doing.

Conclusion

Leaders in the missions ministry of Elmbrook Church have a keen interest in research and appropriate strategies, and they consider that the various kinds of partnerships in ministry have been timely inducements in the missions program. No single fellowship, regardless of size, can address all the needs of world evangelization, but carefully selected relationships can enhance strategic and effective use of resources.

CHAPTER 9

Church-to-Church Group Report

Facilitator: David Mays

Abstract: *This working group addressed church partnerships that work specifically across cultural boundaries to see the Body of Christ established in all parts of the world. Their report relates general principles for establishing church-to-church relationships and presents nine steps that may lead to such partnerships.*

Focus

The topic addressed by this group involved churches in North America partnering with churches elsewhere in the world for the purpose of planting churches in least evangelized areas. The three key elements were:

- partnership: a long-term, reciprocal relationship
- church-to-church: between two local churches in two different cultures
- a specific project: reaching the least evangelized

Legitimate Goals

1. To experience the unity of Christ across cultures. Cross and Crown Community Church in Arlington Heights, Ill., and a sister church in Haiti illustrate this in their experience (see Chapter 7).

2. To educate and motivate participating congregations concerning involvement in biblical missions. Experiences with short-term mission trips show that they do have this impact on local congregations.

3. To share complementary strengths of churches in different cultures for the upbuilding of the individual churches and of Christ's church as a whole.

4. To learn to pray more intelligently and effectively for spiritual needs and world evangelization.

Dynamics of Partnerships

Other dynamics discussed cover a broad variety of areas which may prove helpful to any church considering partnership.

1. Seek a partnership relationship not simply out of whim but on the basis of a sound missions strategy. Partnership should have a biblical basis as a result of thinking through what God has called the church to do in the world.

2. Discern the times. Partnering is already a growing movement among churches. As one man said, "Since I am their leader, I have to catch up with them."

3. Churches need to experience both unity and diversity in the Body. A church should deliberately seek a partner with common concerns. There are bound to be differences (complementary strengths), but there should also be a certain basis of commonality allowing a profitable relationship which accomplishes a mutual goal.

4. This is a "high-touch" era in U. S. culture as the baby boomers in North America come into positions of authority. People desire relationships. In our day, a relational experience can be a driving force for missions.

5. A continued strong missions thrust from North America depends upon getting more individuals and churches involved in cross-cultural relationships.

Developmental Factors

Another topic concerned some of the steps that may lead to church-to-church partnership. What kinds of things are churches doing now or could churches easily do that help develop genuine church-to-church partnerships?

1. Develop a specific missions strategy to maximize the effectiveness, and introduce the concept to the church.

2. Ask the denominational mission board for assistance, or contact nationals through a mission agency with which the church works.

3. Contact nationals through missionaries. Sometimes someone who is involved in a missionary or evangelistic effort in another

culture becomes a member of a particular church. Or missionaries come and ask for prayer for particular individuals or groups they work with. These added factors may introduce a natural relationship which develops in time.

4. Invite a national to visit the church.

5. Learn through a church which is in a partnership.

6. Overseas travelers may make contact through some natural route. Someone on vacation may have been persuaded to visit a mission work, or someone from the church may be sent overseas on some kind of business.

7. Support a national organization or worker. This could provide the basis for the flowering of a partnership.

8. Missionary care groups may go visit missionary work. Many churches have some subgroup within the church, such as a care group or a Sunday School class, with a focus on a particular missionary. As they get interested in that missionary's work, they may visit that field and thus make contact with national workers.

9. Focus on a particular people group and then initiate a plan of action to follow up the prayers.

Steps in Formation

The group also prepared a checklist for churches to use when exploring and establishing a partnership with another church.

1. Do preparatory research. Use all resources available to understand as much as you can, not only about the task you are trying to accomplish, but also the people you are trying to work with. Study the cultures of the sister church and the target people. Learn the sister church's history.

2. Work with a reliable facilitating agent, agency, or association. There was some debate about whether it is necessary for every church to work through a facilitating agency. But generally speaking, this group felt that to maximize the probability of success, groups really need to work through and with people who have had more experience.

3. Seek a partner with common motivation, concerns, and purpose, and agree together on the purpose for the relationship. Be intentionally relational. A partnership should be entered into on the basis of a sound strategy that gives a certain task orientation. But the task orientation of some Western churches can overwhelm more

relational-type people. Identify how the relationship will be reciprocal.

4. Identify the proper representative contact in the sister church.

5. Work under the leadership of a highly committed, relational, knowledgable point person in your church. To avoid as many problems as possible, the person who is the driving force or key contact (on both sides) needs to be someone deeply committed to this experience who has the time and some serious cross-cultural training and experience.

6. Be thorough and patient. Persevere. Plan long-term. Take whatever time and effort necessary to cultivate a solid relationship. Do not be too quick to make judgments.

7. Undergird the effort with prayer. Because of the hazards and the spiritual warfare, any kind of cross-cultural work needs to be undergirded with prayer.

8. Do cross-cultural training of your people. Have Sunday School classes and short-term seminars focused on the topic.

9. Move slowly with regard to finances. Establish policies on funding in advance. Make finances a minor element, and relate them primarily to mutual projects. Learn the difference between appropriate funding projects and those which create dependency or undercut self worth.

10. Never lose sight of the focus which brought about involvement in the first place. Relationships tend to take on a character of their own, and rightfully so, but if the ultimate objective is to reach the world for Christ, then one cannot afford to be sidetracked from that goal.

11. Westerners particularly need to think about key attitudes such as assuming a learner position. If one's own congregation is not experienced cross-culturally, the person in the head position in the partnership is learning a great deal. He or she may then tend to assume everybody else in the church already knows these things when, in reality, they do not. Assume little cross-cultural knowledge.

This group felt that the biblical basis for partnerships in general had already been developed adequately in these sessions. However, some did feel that specific dynamics are at work in the local church which are distinct from the other types of partnerships being addressed. This is suggested as a topic for consideration at a future conference.

Section 4

❖❖❖

Mission-to-Mission Partnerships

Chapter 10

Mission-to-Mission Relationships

Ian M. Hay

Abstract: *A description of the historical relationship between SIM and the forty-year-old Evangelical Mission Society of Nigeria which currently has more than 900 missionaries.*

Introduction

A few years ago, I participated in a consultation in England on the theme of "emerging missions" and their relationship to Western mission societies. One of the major addresses was delivered by Rev. Panya Baba, who was then Director of the Evangelical Missionary Society (EMS) of Nigeria. Even at that time, I deemed it strange to call EMS an emerging mission. Beginning more than 40 years ago and now having 922 missionaries, EMS is larger and older than a majority of Western societies.

Then I went to a consultation in the U.S.A. to discuss "Third-World Missions." That term also has problems. With Western Christians now in the minority, the term we are using here, "Two-Thirds world," is more nearly correct.

Call them what you will, non-Western churches constitute a powerful new factor in reaching the world for Christ. The 200-year-old pattern of Western dominance is broken. If present trends continue, the majority of Christian missionaries will soon be from non-Western countries. Already there are an estimated 36,000 of them. At the present growth rate, there will be well over 160,000 by the year 2000.[1] Western missionaries are currently estimated at 60,000.

Christian missions have always faced a kaleidoscopic future, demanding constant adaptation to change. *The greatest contemporary change facing missions is the church that exists around the world—a church with remarkable strength and growth.* This is not a new phenomenon. However, it is a growing one.

More than fifty years ago, Latourette said, "... increasingly the determining question of all mission programs must be 'What will most contribute to an ongoing Christian community.'"[2]

Any study, then, of the relationship between Western and Two-Thirds world missions must allow for such change. At each stage of the growth of the church, the relationship will differ. Disaster awaits those missions and individual missionaries who either will not or cannot adapt.

In order to understand clearly the relationships between mission and mission, we must understand the relationships which should exist between mission and church. It is valid to ask who is a sending church and who is a receiving church. The receiving church must become a sending church, if it is to be a responsible church — mature before God in the accomplishment of the purposes of God.[3]

In 1971, I chaired the program committee for the IFMA/EFMA consultation held at Green Lake, Wisconsin (GL'71). The affirmation which came out of GL'71 included the following:

"and we confess...

... our failure to work more consistently toward the development of a fully responsible church at home and abroad;

... our tendency towards paternalism, authoritarianism, a lack of trust in our relations with our Christian brethren;

... our slowness in building scriptural bridges of unity and fellowship between North American and overseas churches:

and we therefore urge mission societies...

... to discover forms of church-mission-church relationship that allow for the fullest scriptural expression of the missionary nature and purpose of the church

... to share with their missionaries and their constituencies what is being done around the world to develop new patterns of church-mission-church relations;

... to evaluate their relations with home and overseas churches through fellowship and consultation in biblical and related studies;

... to foster reciprocal ministry between churches at home and overseas on the basis of mutual love, acceptance and oneness in Jesus Christ;..."[4]

SIM took this affirmation seriously. From the beginning, the goal of SIM has been to have a true biblical partnership in all of our church relationships. While we have not always achieved this goal at the grass roots level, still officially this has been the goal. Philippians 1:5 gives the key thought. The Apostle Paul speaks of "your fellowship in the Gospel." The Greek word translated "fellowship" is koinonia. This is often thought of as camaraderie when, in reality, it means "to become a sharer, to be made a partner." Paul is speaking about partnership in the fullest sense of the word.[5]

To understand the relationships, it is helpful to study history. For 200 years the modern missionary movement has been a phenomenal success. The church of our Lord Jesus Christ has become a worldwide reality.

Twenty-five years ago, however, that movement in the West almost came to a standstill in the wake of the demise of colonialism and Western imperialism. Also, as news of dynamic church growth in the Two-Thirds world swept through Western churches, many came to the conclusion that the task was accomplished. Churches were told that missions from the West were a thing of the past. Recruitment sagged. Some mission societies almost went out of business.

That philosophy did not prevail. To the contrary, over the last decade a fresh breath of concern to reach the 3 billion unreached people has swept through the church.

With that concern has come the realization that God is doing some startling things—things that are distinct from traditional patterns. They relate to the roles that non-Western churches are assuming in world evangelism.

SIM

These roles present older missionary societies like SIM with the need to rearrange their thinking and adapt to what is happening.

SIM, begun in 1893 as the Sudan Interior Mission, is in its ninety-eighth year. It is an evangelical, international, interdenominational mission society. Its original statement of mission says:

"The purpose of the Mission is to ... preach the Gospel of the Lord Jesus Christ with the aim of establishing churches which are self-propagating; ..."

The pioneers of SIM had a simple goal. They were challenged to penetrate new territory and to evangelize vast areas then totally untouched. They felt the burden of God to go to the interior of Nigeria with the gospel. They tried to find existing mission societies to send them but were unable to do so. They therefore went on their own with whatever support they could find. Their dependence was solely upon God.

As Dr. Rowland Bingham gathered together others with a similar burden to his, he formed what has become SIM. His first inclination was to make SIM consistent with his own denominational background, which was Canadian Baptist. After much prayer and dependence upon the Holy Spirit, he felt that this was not the direction that he should take. He therefore formed an interdenominational mission.[6]

The pioneers learned quickly as part of their methodology that Christ's total commission demands more than evangelism. To bring people to new birth through evangelism and then stop at that point is to follow a truncated commission. Discipling is crucial—the teaching of the "all things whatsoever I have commanded you." As a result, the original purpose statement has been refined as:

The purpose of SIM is to glorify God
by evangelizing the unreached
and ministering to human need,
discipling believers into churches
equipped to fulfill Christ's Commission.

For a complete understanding of this case study, we must recognize what Bingham's decision meant. SIM is an interdenominational mission for valid reasons. It therefore makes the supporting constituency of SIM a different kind of constituency than it would have been had the Mission been denominational. It also makes the relationships with the churches it founded unique.

This means that ultimately, the way we glorify God is by seeing not only the church come into being, but a particular kind of church; i.e., a reproducing church—a missionary church.[7]

ECWA

In keeping with its goal, SIM was used of God to start, in Nigeria, the Evangelical Church of West Africa (ECWA). In that country, the histories of ECWA and SIM are inseparable. It is true that ECWA did not become a separate legal identity until 1954.

However, I know from personal experience (my parents went to Nigeria with SIM in 1918) that in the minds of the pioneers of SIM there was never a distinction between the purpose of the Mission and the church they were endeavoring to bring into being. The only distinction was organizational. It was recognized that the mission is not the church.

The first established church of a formal nature came in 1908 when the first converts were baptized. That is the true date that ECWA began.

Legal recognition for ECWA was granted by the British Government in Nigeria in 1954, six years before Nigeria became independent. In 1976, SIM transferred full responsibilities for the ministries to ECWA. This transfer has been documented by my colleague, former SIM Deputy General Director W. Harold Fuller.[8]

ECWA is now a mature church, a denomination in Nigeria, with more than 2,200 congregations. She continually assesses her own goals to determine how those fulfill the divine commission. Only in this way will ECWA be able to maintain validity as a mature church.

There are, of course, external problems for ECWA through overt persecution in some places. Some churches have been burned by radical fundamentalist Muslims; pastors have been killed as a result of mob action. Other places have internal problems, either through a lack of moral fiber or through a lack of clear theological understanding. Tribalism causes others to violate the unity of the Spirit. Many are churches of the poor and suffer the frustrations of financial need. ECWA is aware of these problems and her president, Rev. Panya Baba, has issued an urgent call for prayer and revival.

Many people are surprised to learn that tensions also sometimes exist between a mission society and its related churches. SIM is no exception.

That problem often comes in trying to relate the nature of the mission to that of the maturing churches. A mission society, of course, must be true to its nature—it is a religious order, a group of individuals committed to fulfilling corporate goals of evangelism and church planting. Some church leaders have difficulty understanding this. To them the maturing of the church takes precedence over evangelism.

On the other hand, missiologists like Donald McGavran take issue with that philosophy. He spent the best years of his long life challenging missions with the necessity of goal-consciousness for evangelism. He was at it until his recent death. In one of his latest articles, he said:

Helping young churches has become a major concern of many missionary societies. Indeed, for some missionary societies, helping young denominations in Asia, Africa, or Latin America has become the sole purpose of mission. This course of action is defended on the grounds that a church or denomination made up of citizens of that country is much better able to evangelize its unreached peoples than most able missionaries from some other land.

... As long as the contemporary delusion persists that the best missionary work today is helping young denominations, so long will these unreached peoples of earth remain unevangelized.[9]

McGavran's persistent single-mindedness helped keep some Western missions from falling into the trap of denomination-building. For that we are grateful and we would urge others gifted as he was to be "burrs under our saddle" to continue to exercise their gift. This could, however, produce a dichotomy which in itself could be fatal.

In my view, we have had enough debate polarizing evangelism and church development. These two emphasize biblical imperatives from opposite perspectives, both of which are true. The danger of denomination-building is granted and must be studiously avoided. Our generation, however, has the opportunity of working with a vibrant growing church around the world. This is pure pleasure and should be a major part of our methodology for evangelism. We dare not ignore the church.

The growth of the church in the Two-Thirds world, however, does not mean that Western churches and their missionary societies are off the hook. We must commit ourselves to fresh methods to reach unreached peoples. World Christians, wherever they are, must be involved. But this demands of us an acute awareness of our role in regard to the emerging churches and their task in evangelism.

Simplistic answers, then, are not possible. Some leaders feel that in certain places missions should declare a moratorium and move on to new areas. This is a tempting thought for the missions, for the physical privations of pioneering are small matters compared to the "care of all the churches." But as long as there are multitudes on the globe who do not know Jesus Christ as Lord and Savior, it is ridiculous to speak of withdrawing all missionaries and all mission finances so the church can "fulfill itself independently." SIM and ECWA agree on that.

There are also problems of mushrooming growth. ECWA is growing numerically so rapidly that the leaders are frightened at the large numbers of untaught Christians and the potential for spiritual weakness. When I asked the elders of a particular ECWA church why they still felt the need for Western missionaries, they immediately responded, "for teaching."

The first item on the agenda of our meetings with the trustees of ECWA was their desire to see seminary training upgraded to post-graduate level. They are asking us to help bring that to fruition.

Three years ago, my wife and I were in Nigeria as the special guests of ECWA. Two messages came through to us loud and clear: One, the church is strong, and two, the relationship between SIM and ECWA is excellent. The expressions of love and joy which poured out everywhere were an eloquent statement of thankfulness to God and love for the missionaries who brought them the gospel.

In the messages I gave to ECWA leaders, I used the apostle Paul's words to the Thessalonians: "You are our crown, our joy, and our hope," emphasizing that SIM looks on ECWA in that way.

ECWA need never feel threatened that SIM is trying to run its show. With ECWA, nationalization is a fait accompli. It has been more than 15 years since SIM transferred the responsibility for directing SIM ministries in Nigeria. Since then both SIM and ECWA have realized the need for constant review of our relationships.

But one of the functions of a mission society is stimulation, a word that comes from the Latin, stimulare, "to goad, as in herding animals." Even as Paul and his compatriots had a ministry to the early church in two directions, so we are to arouse churches, both at home and abroad.

The New Testament teaches us that for a church to be truly church, it must be concerned for the whole world. The dynamic of a New Testament church was a vigorous missionary outreach. Paul honored the church at Thessalonica for that. He said, "From you sounded out the word of the Lord" (I Thess. 1:8). Jesus said that the evidence of a Spirit-empowered life was to witness both in Jerusalem, Judea, Samaria, and to the uttermost part of the world (Acts 1:8). It wasn't either/or; it was both/and.

Any discussion of this nature must speak to the subject of indigeneity. I have stated that ECWA is a mature, responsible church. To be a responsible church is to be indigenous, and ECWA fits that description. But that needs definition. Harvey Conn pinpoints the problem when he says, "Mission vocabulary coins its new words— 'indigenous church' in the latter half of the nineteenth century, 'indigenization' in the 1950s, 'contextualization' in the 1970s."[10] And I suppose I can add, "partnering" in the 1990s. The term indigenous, because of both misuse and overuse, has fallen upon hard times. Some seem to confuse the term with nationalization, while others limit its usage to financial matters only. Both of these are a mistake.

In SIM, we believe that it is our responsibility to plant a church which is allowed to grow in its own soil and come to full flower there. And that includes its missionary obligation. As long as the church is built solidly upon the foundation of Jesus Christ (1 Cor. 3:11) and as long as it follows sound biblical principles, there is no reason why it cannot develop practices which differ in some respects from churches elsewhere.

One of the distinct advantages that an interdenominational mission has is that it is under no obligation to reproduce a church structure and polity exactly like structures elsewhere in the world. There are, of course, problems inherent in practicing this principle. Through the years SIM has been learning and growing along with the church. One thing we have learned is that our relationships with national churches are dynamic. Changing patterns, growth, and maturity demand flexibility. There is not one fixed relationship that will apply at all times and in all places.

Dr. Peter Cotterell, former SIM missionary and now president of London Bible College, England, pointed out the difficulties a mission society faces in relation to a truly indigenous church.

> SIM has tried to emphasize Bible teaching, so the churches will have leaders who can be relied on to lead the churches biblically. But the missionary can neither force a teaching on an autonomous church, nor compel it to abandon some principle.
>
> ... In an indigenous church the missionary cannot forbid. He can advise, he can exhort, he can teach, he can plead, but he can't forbid.
>
> ... The point is that an independent church has to be free to make its own decisions. A 40- or 50-year-old baby is quite a load to carry on your back—and the baby objects to the indignity of it. SIM does not try to dominate the churches, but to work with them in partnership. Church leaders will often ask for advice from us, but in the end, the decision is theirs.[11]

SIM has always followed the policy of indigeneity. The church must be responsible and mature, well grounded in the Scriptures, capable of continuing growth and reaching out to others. The fact that ECWA is a responsible church is not an accident. The founding of ECWA was the fulfillment of early SIM policies. It is the outgrowth of the pioneers' methodology followed by godly African leaders.

> "Looking beyond the preaching of the gospel, Dr. Bingham and the leaders of SIM saw their ultimate goal — the establishment of the church in Africa."[12]

SIM pioneers began the work in the "indigenous church principles" stage Conn referred to. From the beginning the writings of John Nevius and Roland Allen were studied and applied to the Nigerian scene. Furthermore, they were working in the area where Henry Venn, nineteenth-century General Secretary of the Church Missionary Society, had his greatest impact. All missionaries in West Africa owe Venn a debt. Venn is a "legendary figure in Protestant mission. He exerted a powerful influence in shaping the common pattern of the missionary enterprise through the nineteenth century, an influence that continued in considerable measure right down to the middle of the twentieth century."[13]

The work of SIM in Nigeria which resulted in ECWA and EMS was affected profoundly by Venn's ideas. It was Venn who, along with American Congregationalist missionary Rufus Anderson,[14] first defined the three signs of church maturity as self-support, self-government, and self-extension.

It is recognized that whereas this "three self" concept was a reaction to the paternalistic attitudes of the colonial era, it was, however, only a beginning to what is a "dynamic process."[15]

The church in South Korea is another outstanding example of the value of these principles.[16] Similarly both ECWA in Nigeria and the Kale Heywet Church in Ethiopia are further proof of the validity of their correct usage.

That there have been excessive practices arising out of this concept which have led to error and weakening of the church cannot be denied. Witness the problems brought about in China with the government's control of the church through a corruption of the three-self concept. Beyerhaus warns that an overzealous use of his formula can be devastating to the development of the church. He feels that the "self" emphasis raises serious biblical questions.[17]

In 1965, at the IFMA annual meeting, I read a paper in which I pointed out the danger of overemphasis on indigenous principles which results in misjudgment and misunderstanding between missionaries and local churches. I stated:

> ... Misunderstanding the full meaning of indigenous church principles has caused missionaries and missions to establish such a separation between missions and church that isolation results and scriptural fellowship is lacking ... a gulf arises between missionaries and the church, and ultimately between the mission organization and the church ... the pendulum

swings too far. Instead of domination there is isolation. Instead of overinfluencing the church, there is fear of speaking out at all.

The result is that missionaries feel they have no part in the church, and then they become critical of obvious weaknesses within the church. In turn the church is critical of the missionaries for their lack of understanding and concern. The result is division, heartache, disillusion. Neither Roland Allen nor St. Paul wanted this to happen.[18]

In spite of these and other difficulties, indigenous policies correctly applied have proven themselves to be sound. ECWA is one proof of this. The work was founded and maintained along with principles as adapted to fit the local scene.

The question of finance seems to dominate any discussion of indigenous church policies. SIM has always recognized that the financial needs in a rapidly expanding church cannot be ignored. There are legitimate areas of help. The problem is always to locate that fine line between worthwhile and needful assistance without at the same time taking away from the church its own sense of responsibility. Any semblance of economic imperialism or colonialism will harm, not help, the church. That must be avoided.

Special care is needed in giving financial help. John Janzen has warned,

> Whenever generosity of giving, teaching, and helping is of an unconditional character, the recipient must be able to return the gift of some equivalent in order to remain his own respectable self. Otherwise he will begin seeing himself as inferior to the giver; his personal sense of worth is downgraded and instead of being grateful he will be bitter. This set of forces is very much misunderstood in many mission programs today.[19]

Whenever there is partnership, the quantity that each partner brings to the relationship varies. At different stages in the development of the church the needs will vary. There are times when it is legitimate for SIM and its supporting constituency to assist a financially weaker church in the same way that the young churches in the first century assisted the church in Jerusalem (1 Cor. 16:3). True, that case differed in that it was the new churches helping the old. Nevertheless, the principle was the same for it was those who had, helping those who did not have.

Included in SIM's strategy for Nigeria are the following goals for outreach:

1. to have an increased missionary involvement in the Evangelism and Church Growth Department
2. to assist in developing an integrated team approach in new areas as well as church areas
3. to participate in urban evangelism
4. to assist in missionary training for cross-cultural and foreign mission work
5. to assist EMS in expansion

Part of SIM's goal in Nigeria, therefore, has been to establish a responsible church that is outgoing in its witness, and to help provide the leadership training and biblical stimulation that brings about its aggressive evangelism.

EMS

That three billion people in the world have no near neighbor to tell them of Christ is mind-boggling. Obviously if anything is to be accomplished, it must be broken down into bite-size chunks.

Mobilizing all Christians to this task is beyond imagination. This too must be broken down into meaningful terms. I make no pretense of devising a strategy to reach the three billion unreached peoples. This study is limited to an analysis of two societies; one foreign (SIM) and one national (EMS) within the context of one country—Nigeria— and relating in differing ways with one denomination—ECWA.

God uses people to do his work. These people, however, do not function independently nor operate in a vacuum. God has always put these individual Christians together into meaningful units which have functioned either as local congregations or as missionary bands, religious orders, or mission societies.

Over the years some have questioned the validity of mission societies like SIM or EMS. They state that it is an accident of history; that if local churches had performed as they ought, there would be no need for such societies. I do not agree with this. It is clear that God raised up mission societies to accomplish His purposes. The evident blessing of God upon them makes it very difficult for one to believe that the structure of the organization took God by surprise.

History tells us that structures for missions have, by and large, always been greeted with reluctance and questioned by formal church governments. This was evident in the early church as evidenced in the necessity for Paul to defend his own ministry. It was this that forced the pioneers of SIM to establish the Mission as a separate organization in order to accomplish God's will.

The Bible gives principles which apply to each generation. The earliest evidence of what has become the modern missionary society is to be found in the New Testament among the apostles. Paul and Barnabas, Barnabas and Mark, Paul, Silas, Timothy, and Luke are combinations similar to today's societies.

When he was Home Director for Overseas Missionary Fellowship, Dr. Arthur F. Glasser said,

> "The New Testament distinguishes between structured local congregations (churches) and structured apostolic bands called by God to evangelize the heathen and plant new churches. Whereas the Apostles were of the Church, their corporate ministry of missionary outreach necessitated among themselves patterns of leadership and organization, recruitment and finance, training and discipline distinct from comparable patterns within local congregations. This significant distinction gives Biblical sanction to today's missionary fellowships."[20]

Dr. Ralph Winter has emphasized the need for two types of organizations within the church. He calls one group "sodalities (that is, other structured, decentralized, and especially voluntary initiatives) which are distinct from organizational modalities, (that is, overall, given, governmental structures)."[21]

By these definitions SIM is a sodality—a religious order within historic Protestantism. While it is separate by its structure and inter-denominational character from more organized church structures (modalities), it is part and parcel of the body of Christ, but as a sodality, not a modality. It has, through the years, gained certain distinctive skills in the cross-cultural missionary enterprise which it has utilized for the glory of God.

Since the beginning of church history, then, there have been missionary societies or religious orders similar to SIM and EMS. These groups have functioned as distinct from the corporate structures of churches. At the same time, they have recognized that they belong organically together with the local church.

Dr. George W. Peters said:

As long as there is a need for missionaries and such are available, and as long as the churches and/or individual men will retain the missionary vision and passion, so long will there be a need for missionary sending agencies. However, the missionary, the local congregation, and the missionary society belong organically together and must function in a harmonious cooperative manner to further the work of God, whether bound together organizationally or not.[22]

SIM was used of God to develop in Nigeria, EMS, which is also a sodality. However, unlike SIM after which it was patterned, it is an integral part of ECWA which is a modality.

In 1948, the SIM West Africa Field Council established what was called Jamiyyar Masu Bishara na S.I.M. cikin Afrika ta Yamma (the S.I.M. Evangelists' Society of West Africa). The name was later changed to African Missionary Society which, in turn, has grown into EMS, the missionary arm of ECWA.

For the first seven years or so, an SIM missionary actually functioned as secretary for the mission and helped them work through the dynamics of how they wanted to function. Then a Nigerian was appointed.

EMS has developed into a vibrant missionary agency. In 1972, I published a description of the development of this society, which then had one hundred missionaries and an annual unsubsidized budget of over $20,000.[23]

Since then the work has grown markedly. Today EMS has more than 900 missionaries supported for the most part by ECWA churches. They also receive financial assistance from SIM, Partners, Hilfe fur Bruder, and other similar agencies.

Since its inception, the concept of EMS has been missionary, as distinct from local evangelists. That is, by definition, only those who were cross-cultural in their missionary outreach could be a part of the organization.

The fact is, however, that EMS has reached mainly ECWA's "Judea and Samaria." Presently they have one couple working with African expatriates in London, with negotiations underway for another to work in Chicago. Apart from these, the farthest any missionary has gone is Ghana, and even there he was a missionary to the Hausa people living as expatriates in Accra. Panya Baba has spoken of this forcefully to the ECWA General Church Council. SIM and EMS are determined to find ways to help ECWA become a church for the whole world.

Laborers Together

There are three models for SIM partnership with EMS. Model one is to help EMS in practical ways as was done when EMS sent its missionary to Ghana. EMS supported the missionary by prayer and finance. SIM assisted in the transportation costs and provided liaison in Ghana. SIM missionaries in Ghana encouraged and assisted the EMS missionary. At all times, however, the complete responsibility and authority for the missionary was retained by EMS.

This model worked also when EMS missionaries worked in close association with SIM missionaries in Northern Nigeria, Benin, and Niger Republic. Although in this model there are potential problems, it has worked well in practice and should continue to do so. Legal problems with fund transfers do affect EMS but when legal ways can be found for SIM to assist in fund transfers for workers assigned to countries contiguous to Nigeria, this is the best model, allowing EMS to provide on-the-spot supervision.

Model two may be better when missionaries are to be sent to countries farther afield. By this, SIM and EMS could enter into an agreement whereby EMS missionaries, who are called of God to work in countries other than Nigeria or its immediate environs, may be seconded to SIM for work in other countries where SIM is working.

SIM accepts missionaries from anywhere in the world who meet all candidate requirements, regardless of their nationality. The only restriction is that those missionaries must perform their cross-cultural ministry in countries other than their own. This restriction strengthens and protects the church. In SIM's view, it is wrong to siphon off the cream and leave the church with skim milk. Hence, for example, well-qualified nationals have been a part of ECWA and EMS leadership in Nigeria and not members of SIM.

However, there is no reason why a qualified Nigerian could not be a part of SIM, supported by ECWA (with outside assistance where needed) to work in Chicago or Pakistan. In saying this, I do not wish to imply an exaltation of SIM, nor do I wish to depreciate EMS.

On one occasion I suggested this model to the late Dr. Byang Kato whose immediate response was to inquire why they should join SIM. The problem is administrative. The logistics and oversight needed may be beyond EMS's strength at this time. As EMS and SIM work together in true partnership, ECWA will thus be able to become a church concerned for the whole world.

SIM already has working agreements of this nature with churches in other lands that fit this model. For many years, German missionaries have worked with SIM. They are members of SIM and qualify in every way as any other SIM missionary. In Germany, however, they are members of and are supported by Deutsche Missions Gemeinschaft (DMG) or one of the other partner missions in Germany. This has created no problems either in Germany or in our fields. We have a true partnership.

Similar agreements have been worked out with two denominations in Korea. There are now 31 Koreans who are full members of SIM but who, in Korea, are under the care and discipline of their home denominations.

SIM and EMS are working toward a similar agreement which would allow applicants who meet SIM qualifications and who feel called of God to service beyond Nigeria to join EMS, be supported by ECWA, and then be seconded to SIM for service assignment.

While they are on their assigned field of service, they would be members of SIM and subject to SIM leadership just as any other SIM missionary and would qualify for leadership in SIM as well. When they are on furlough in Nigeria, they would be fully EMS in the same sense that DMG missionaries are in Germany or Korean missionaries are when on furlough in Korea. Their deputation would be as EMS missionaries.

Their ministry outside Nigeria would be in accord with EMS and ECWA goals for outreach but would be under SIM. EMS is seriously seeking to answer a call to ethnic ministries in Chicago following this pattern.

Model three has yet to be developed. It is for SIM to assist EMS in answering the call of God to areas where SIM does not minister. In these cases SIM would seek to assist EMS to fulfill God's call without the need for SIM involvement, as far as the missionaries are concerned. The help SIM would give would be logistical and SIM would assist as a facilitator, but the responsibilities and authority would belong totally to EMS.

Conclusion

Most international missions are confederations of various nationalities, each segregated to its own area or work. SIM seeks to integrate all nationalities into a common work force. We have Africans, Asians, Europeans, North Americans, and Australasians working together.

Tensions are not unknown when language, social perspectives, and cultural behavior patterns do not jibe. There can be a tendency to feel that one's own ways are somehow superior. Grace is needed for each to understand and accept the other and enjoy true harmony. This grace of acceptance is needed throughout the entire body of Christ. Western churches, which have long enjoyed the "prestige" of being the leaders in world evangelism, must come to grips with the fact that God uses whom He will to achieve His goals.

This case study of SIM, ECWA, and EMS may help to determine strategy whereby SIM and EMS can contribute strength to each other. This should exemplify partnering in the truest sense.

They have worked together in the past and will continue to do so. The original goal of SIM, for example, was the huge Hausa nation situated mainly in Northern Nigeria. The pioneers never reached that goal even though they prayed, strategized, and labored for it. Only within the last fifteen years have we begun to see the fruition—and that as a result of the outreach of EMS.[24]

A major part of any missionary methodology has to be tied to the churches God has raised up around the world. The establishment of Two-Thirds world missions and their proliferation is a giant strategic tool in the hands of the Holy Spirit. The only way that the unreached of the world will be reached is for the total church to be mobilized.

We must be careful, however, not to come to the same kind of mistaken conclusion that was made in the 1960s. We must not infer that since God is raising up non-Western missionaries that we are not needed in the task. Our Lord wills to use all parts of His body in taking the gospel to every creature. This being true, the measure of a mission's effectiveness, it seems to me, is the production of an outgoing, witnessing church—a church concerned for the whole world and one that reproduces itself.

Any mission which has not developed churches concerned for evangelism should repent. Diligent study is needed to determine ways in which the young churches can expand their vision beyond their own national boundaries. Older missions should find ways to help the younger ones, without damaging either their indigeneity or effectiveness. In this way, both older and younger missions will fulfill their God-given responsibilities in true partnership.

Endnotes

[1] Larry D. Pate, *From Every People*, (Monrovia, CA: MARC, 1989), 17, 44.

[2] Kenneth Scott Latourette, *Missions Tomorrow*, (New York: Harper and Brothers, 1936), 127-131.

[3] Ian M. Hay, "Church/Missionary/Mission Relationships," *Missions in Creative Tension*, ed. Vergil Gerber, (South Pasadena, CA: William Carey Library, 1971), 84-94.

[4] "A Green Lake '71 Affirmation," *Missions in Creative Tension*, The Green Lake '71 Compendium, ed. Vergil Gerber, (South Pasadena: William Carey Library, 1971), 383.

[5] George W. Peters, *A Biblical Theology of Missions*, (Chicago: Moody Press, 1972), 234.

[6] Rowland V. Bingham, *Seven Sevens of Years*, (Toronto: Evangelical Publishers, 1943), 110-114.

[7] For a more detailed understanding of what makes SIM what it is, see Ian M. Hay, *Foundations: Scriptural Principles Undergirding SIM*, (Charlotte, NC: SIM International, 1988).

[8] W. Harold Fuller, *Mission-Church Dynamics*, (Pasadena: William Carey Library, 1980).

[9] Donald McGavran, "New Terms to Clarify the Task," *Global Church Growth*, XIX, No. 4 (July-August 1982), 205.

[10] Charles H. Kraft and Tom N. Wisley, *Readings in Dynamic Indigeneity*, (Pasadena: William Carey Library, 1979), xvi.

[11] Peter Cotterell, "Who Calls the Shots?" *Africa Now*, (September-October 1975), 7.

[12] J. H. Hunter, *A Flame of Fire*, (Toronto: Sudan Interior Mission, 1961), 240.

[13] Max Warren, *To Apply the Gospel*, (Grand Rapids: William B. Eerdmans Publishing Company, 1971), 7.

[14] R. Pierce Beaver, *To Advance the Gospel: Selections from the Writings of Rufus Anderson*, (Grand Rapids: William B. Eerdmans Publishing Co., 1967).

[15] Kraft and Wisley, *Readings in Dynamic Indigeneity*, xxix.

[16] T. Stanley Soltau, *Missions at the Crossroads*, (Grand Rapids: Baker Book House, 1954).

[17] Peter Beyerhaus, "The Three Selves Formula—Is it Built on Biblical Foundations?" *Readings in Dynamic Indigeneity*, 15-30.

[18] Ian M. Hay, "Balanced Perspectives," IFMA Annual Meeting, 1965, (Mimeographed).

[19] As quoted in Levi O. Keidel, Jr., "The Peril of Giving," *World Vision Magazine,* November 1971, 8.

[20] "The 'New' Overseas Missionary Fellowship," (unpublished study paper prepared for the OMF, 1965).

[21] "Protestant Mission Societies: the American Experience," *Missiology,* 7, (April 1979), 142-43.

[22] George W. Peters, *A Biblical Theology of Missions,* (Chicago: Moody Press, 1972), 234.

[23] Ian M. Hay, "Emergence of a Missionary-Minded Church in Nigeria," *Missions in Creative Tension,* ed. by Vergil Gerber, (Pasadena: William Carey Library, 1971), 84-95. See also Ian M. Hay, "Relationship between SIM International and the Evangelical Missionary Society," (D.Miss. dissertation, Trinity Evangelical Divinity School, Deerfield, Il.).

[24] Ian M. Hay, "Relationship between SIM International and the Evangelical Missionary Society," (D. Miss. dissertation, Trinity Evangelical Divinity School, Deerfield, Il.), 1-59.

CHAPTER 11

A Two-Thirds World Perspective: A Case Study

Panya Baba

Abstract: *The president of the Evangelical Church of West Africa stresses the need for mission-to-mission partnerships to accomplish the unfinished task of world evangelization. He describes a number of partnership models already in action and presents some future plans for such relationships.*

> *"Two can accomplish more than twice as much as one, for the results can be much better. And one standing alone can be attacked and defeated, but two can stand back to back and conquer. Three is even better, for triple braided cord is not easily broken,"* Eccles. 4:9,12 (Living Bible).
>
> *"For we are partners working together for God and you are God's field,"* I Cor. 3:9 (Good News Today).

According to Dr. David Barrett, working in isolation was one of the primary reasons for the failure of past generations to complete world evangelization. Therefore we need to consider cooperation and partnership more seriously.

The unfinished task of world evangelization in our generation is still a great challenge. No one church or mission organization can finish the task alone. In some areas, great need has already led to partnerships. Below is a description of a few of these models.

Partnership Models
Three-Party Partnership Model—
EMS, SIM, and the Good News Church in Ghana

Around 1974 the Church in Ghana invited the Evangelical Missionary Society of the Evangelical Church of West Africa (EMS of ECWA) to send Hausa-speaking missionaries for outreach work among the thousands of Hausa-speaking people in Ghana.

After several years of prayer, EMS accepted the call. But it was found that the support of a missionary couple and the traveling expenses involved would be more than twice the support for a couple in Nigeria. Though EMS was willing to send the couple, it became impossible to raise enough support to cover all of their expenses.

Because of this, a three-party partnership was formed. EMS provided the missionaries and their support. The church in Ghana provided the accommodation, and SIM provided the travel expenses and means of transportation. This model helped a lot to start evangelism and church planting among the Hausa people until the time when the indigenous converts had been trained and took over the ministry. Without such cooperation and partnership, the two churches planted through this outreach might not exist today.

Partnership between a Church in Zaire, the Church of the Province in Kenya, and a Church Overseas

During the 1985 International Consultation on Missions held in Nigeria, Dr. Tukumbo Adeyemo shared with us an example of a three-party partnership.

The church in Zaire had a need for pastors and teachers in the Kiswahili-speaking area of eastern Zaire. Because of the language barrier, the church there had difficulty communicating the Gospel to them. Therefore they approached their sister Church of Province in Kenya for partnership. The church in Kenya sent the missionaries. The supervision was done by the church in Zaire. An appeal was made to the Episcopal Church in the West to subsidize the support and other missionary expenses.

Again cooperation and partnership promoted the work of the Lord and resulted in reaching people. The problem with this type of partnership where *total* financial support comes from the West is that should the finances from the West cease, the project may suffer.

Partnership between In Contact Ministries, EMS of ECWA, and Tear Fund

The EMS of ECWA was invited by In Contact Ministries in London to send a missionary couple for evangelism and church planting among the African students and the black and white communities of East London.

After several years of prayer, EMS accepted the invitation. The partnership agreement and policies were established. Due to the devaluation of Nigerian currency (Naira), it was impossible for EMS to raise the support for the couple and their children living in London.

In Contact Ministries also could not raise the support alone. Therefore a three-party partnership resulted. EMS, assisted by SIM, provided the missionary couple and the airfares. In Contact Ministries is responsible for accommodation and supervision of the work and Tear Fund provides the support in London.

Two-party Partnership between EMS and "X" Organization

Due to a particular Muslim group of people having their own specific beliefs and Arabic language, it was difficult to find the right missionaries in Nigeria to reach them.

EMS became aware of the need to invite "X" organization to evangelize that special group and began working on a partnership agreement with that organization. "X" sent two missionary couples to Nigeria to work with EMS. EMS/ECWA provides the accommodation, means of transportation, and supervision while "X" organization provides the support. The couples are now studying the local language, and we are praying that they will begin ministry soon.

Cooperation in Literature Ministry for Muslim Evangelism

The Call of Hope in Germany, an organization producing literature for Muslim Evangelism, receives hundreds of responses from Nigeria as a result of their literature distribution. They have found it difficult to do adequate follow-up from Germany. They contacted EMS/SIM for cooperation. The Call of Hope provides the literature while the translation, distribution, and follow-up is done by EMS/SIM in Nigeria. This kind of partnership reduces the high cost of postage and allows for easier follow-up within the country.

Cooperation and Partnership in Outreach among Boko people

About 8 to 10 years ago, an SIM missionary in Benin Republic did a survey among the Boko people who were divided by the national boundary between Nigeria and Benin Republic. As a result, he found 15,000 or more Boko people in Nigeria along the border. Although there was no formal, written agreement, he shared the information with EMS.

When I first visited the areas, I found there was not one missionary sharing the Gospel with the Boko people on the Nigerian side. We started sending missionary couples to evangelize the Boko people, but we were handicapped by lack of language to communicate the Gospel to them. The SIM missionary in Benin had gone far in studying the language and even had messages by Boko believers on cassette.

Cooperation and partnership came as a result of the burden for the Boko people. The SIM missionary contributed a lot in providing Gospel cassettes for our missionaries who had not yet learned the language. He also made arrangements for our missionaries to spend time in Benin learning the language. Along with these things, he provided some first-aid medicines for both the missionaries and people of the communities. As a result of this kind of partnership and cooperation, there are approximately 25 churches established on both sides of the border. The work continues to expand there among the Boko and also the Kambari people.

Cooperation in Training

One of the greatest needs for emerging missions in Africa today is for practical, cross-cultural training for our missionaries. We discovered this need as our mission vision increased and the demand for cross-cultural missionaries became so great. There was not only the demand for more missionaries, but also great needs for training those answering the call.

For example, in Nigeria, hundreds of young graduates of institutions of higher learning who received the missionary call demonstrated their zeal and burden for mission. Although they were highly qualified as far as academic education is concerned, they were limited in missionary training. We found it difficult to get adequate practical missionary training for them. It seemed that most of the teaching about missions in our theological institutions was on the history of missions.

This situation was discussed at the Nigeria Evangelical Missions Association, and we realized the need to establish a training center for mission candidates. The individual mission societies who felt the need found it difficult to upgrade their small training program to meet the needs. Working alone they found they could not get enough qualified, experienced missionary teachers and the written materials that would be needed. Finally, it was decided that a partnership effort should be made to see that a training school was established.

This consultation started between the emerging missions themselves, but later they became aware of the need for partnership with traditional missions to share their experience, expertise, and skills in establishing such a training school. Several traditional mission organizations were approached for partnership.

SIM and United Missionary Church Association (UMCA) became the first interested parties, and they gave real encouragement for this partnership to help establish the Nigeria Evangelical Missionary Institute (NEMI) under the umbrella of Nigeria Evangelical Missions

Association (NEMA). The Baptist Mission later developed an interest for cooperation in NEMA projects and is now contributing in several areas, especially in the NEMA Research Project mentioned later.

In the partnership agreement, SIM seconded an experienced missionary couple, Rev. and Mrs. Wilbur O'Donovan, who devoted their time to initiate this training. Rev. O'Donovan also became the first NEMI Coordinator.

SIM also sent Dr. and Mrs. W. Kornfield two different times to hold courses with some experienced Nigerian missionaries on cross-cultural evangelism and church planting. The courses were later adapted by Nigerian missionaries and printed in a book called *Cross-Cultural Christianity*. The Hausa version is now being printed as well.

While SIM was contributing her own part, the UMCA also seconded Miss Lois Fuller who became the first NEMI Dean. She has contributed much to the development of the school, especially after Rev. and Mrs. O'Donovan left Nigeria for furlough. Miss Fuller has put together other practical material into the book, *Going To The Nations*. Her contribution to missionary training in Nigeria cannot be forgotten. UMCA also rented us a part of their mission station as a temporary site to hold the school. We have been operating at the temporary site since about 1986. We have a permanent site near Abuja, the new Federal Capitol Territory in Nigeria, and we will build as the Lord provides funds.

Traditional missionaries and Two-Thirds world missionaries have been working together, teaching courses and contributing in different ways for the success of NEMI. Contributions have come from both traditional and emerging missions to meet the school expenses. Although some mission agencies still have some orientation and seminars for their own missionaries, NEMI has become a cooperative effort for about ten emerging missions for providing training for field missionaries.

Partnership in Research Programs

Research is another project that needs partnership. This need became clear to the Nigeria Evangelical Missions Association when we discovered the need to revise and update the unreached people groups and their locations in the country. Research is highly expensive, and it was impossible for one mission organization to do it all alone. A partnership effort became necessary, and as a result, each emerging mission group in the country seconded one missionary who attended a training course. After the training, the missionaries became resource people for the project.

However, NEMA was left with the problem of how to get equipment needed for the project. Contact was made with a partner organization in Canada, and a computer was donated to handle the research data. As a result of partnership and cooperation, the first volume of the research information has been printed in a book called *A Nation to Win.*

While research continues in Nigeria, broader research is being planned for other African countries through the AEAM Evangelism and Mission Commission. The Executive Committee decided that we would contact one of the traditional missions to ask for secondment of a missionary to coordinate the project in Africa.

Partnership in Exchanging Teachers for Cross-Fertilization

The Korean mission organizations are now sending missionaries to countries around the world including Indonesia, Europe, Africa, and Latin America. Because of the many cultural differences in all of these countries, the Korean organizations are trying to give excellent cross-cultural training to their missionaries.

In 1987 the fifteenth Summer Institute of World Mission in Seoul Korea invited Luis Bush, Peter Octavianus, and me to participate in their summer missionary training program. We spent two weeks on issues of cross-cultural evangelism related to South America, Indonesia, and Africa. The missionary candidates who would be going to those particular areas of the world were given good exposure to the prospective countries. We also were able to learn about Korean cultural differences. This partnership in exchanging teachers for cross-fertilization should be explored further and encouraged more.

Future Partnership Plans

1. **Muslim evangelism:** Muslims are the greatest unreached people groups in North Africa and other Black African countries. Consultation and planning have been going on concerning how to cooperate in special training for Muslim evangelism. The coordinators for such a project are now being considered. Information centers will be set up. A joint effort to mobilize professionals and tent-making missionaries for restricted countries is being planned. And an exchange of missionaries among Two-Thirds world countries is being considered.

2. **Resistant People:**

a) Kanuri people who live in East/North of Nigeria: Consultation and seminars are being held by traditional and emerging missions to share and discuss new ideas as well as obstacles of the Gospel among the Kanuri people. PROCMURA (Project for Christian Muslim Relations) is doing a lot to coordinate this project.

b) Fulani evangelism: Several projects for Fulani outreach are being done in partnership between traditional and emerging missions; for example, the international and regional annual Fulani conferences. Many Fulani are brought to these conferences for evangelism and discipleship. As a result, new converts are taught and motivated to continue with evangelism.

Radio, literature, and cassette ministries are receiving cooperative effort. The exchange of teachers for seminars is bringing about cross-fertilization. Because Fulani are scattered across West Africa, a new proposal has been made to open a coordinating office for Fulani evangelism in West Africa. In such an office, strategy and planning for Fulani outreach would be made together by both traditional and Two-Thirds world missions.

Conclusion

I have mentioned several partnerships which already exist and which are helpful in reaching different groups with the Gospel. We can continue to form such partnerships.

However, I suggest that this consultation explore the possibilities for partnership between mission and mission, especially to reach restricted or closed countries. There are many countries which may not accept missionaries from certain countries but where other countries might be welcomed. For example, some countries are more open to people from Africa or Asia or Latin America than from the West. However, the government foreign exchange restrictions cannot allow these countries to send out money to support their missionaries outside their countries. Is there any solution to this problem?

I would like to see research launched to determine needs and obtain accurate information on restricted or closed countries. We need this data to see what kind of missionaries and what kind of approach will best fit in these countries.

Since we have one Christ and one Gospel, the challenge is ours to explore all possibilities for partnership to insure that we do our part in taking the Gospel to those cut off from the traditional mission approach. My prayer is that this will not be just a consultation on partnership but that it will result in action which will lead to new territory being conquered and that the Gospel message of salvation will be available to many people who would otherwise have no opportunity to hear.

CHAPTER 12

Mission-to-Mission Group Report

Facilitator: John Kyle

Abstract: *A discussion of mission-to-mission relationships addressing such issues as definitions, attitudes, principles, models, and types of partnerships.*

Definitions

Old definitions are breaking down. Mission today requires new definitions. It includes:

- Traditional and nontraditional agencies
- Western and non-Western agencies
- North and South agencies
- Sending and nonsending agencies
- Local churches and individuals

We need to acknowledge "oneness" with many individual "members." And we need to get away from the idea that there are the "haves" and the "have nots." For further research, *Paradigm Shifts in Theology of Missions* by David Bosch is recommended.

Attitudes

The area of attitudes is so fundamental when it comes to partnership. Perhaps a paradigm shift is even taking place in attitudes regarding partnership these days. Partnership is a given. The "going-it-alone" spirit is simply not an option today.

In that spirit, **vulnerability** needs to be understood in any partnershipping effort—being willing to take a risk and enter into new relationships. Just this morning Rudy Giron of the COMIBAM movement suggested a new partnership way that we could relate to what they are doing in Latin America. That kind of spirit needs to be present.

One member said he was approached about a partnership option where he had to say, "We as a mission have never done that before. But we're willing to try." So they entered into a new way of doing partnershipping. Apparently the individual who originally requested this effort had approached other mission agencies and they said, "Well, we just do not do that in our mission." That was the beginning and end of the discussion. When we talk about partnership today, we need to be willing to attempt new relationships.

Commitment is needed on both sides to make a partnership work. We do not have a lot of history or models that we can look to and say, "Hey, this is the way it's going to work out." **Patience** is needed and a commitment to work through the misunderstandings and the tough process of building relationships.

Then there is the need for a **spirit of equality.** Many times when we talk about partnership, it is like someone saying, "I have this home that I am living in, and you're without a home. You can come live in my home." But that is not a partnership. Partnership is not just having someone come and join your team. Partnership is a recognition that multiple parties are bringing important resources for the benefit of all. Both sides also come with needs. And those needs and resources must be understood by all partners so that each side will have something to contribute and something to gain. Until that understanding is achieved, the spirit of equality probably is not possible.

An attitude of equality then results in a **spirit of sharing.** Yours is ours and ours is yours. This is not always easy to do, but that spirit needs to be there.

One of our people shared that he walked into a donor's office and presented two proposals, each for $100,000. The donor liked them and funded them. Unfortunately, both of those proposals were for other agencies and not for the agency this man represented. Afterwards the donor said to him, "I accept both of these, but you know I only have $200,000 to give away this year. Sorry you don't get anything." Not many executives in the past have taken that kind of attitude when it comes to approaching donors, but this genuine spirit of sharing is beginning to characterize new perspectives on partnership.

Closely related is the necessity for **cooperation**—a spirit of working together. This is indispensable, and a spirit of cooperation often leads to tangible partnership.

A concept that comes up again and again is the word trust—**trust and appreciation.** This doesn't just happen. It has to be developed. In our love relationships with spouses, love still has to be processed and worked out in a spirit of trust and appreciation. So it is in partnerships—they must be characterized by love.

Then there is the whole matter of forgiveness—giving and receiving. Anyone who has been involved in any kind of relationship realizes that one has to learn how to forgive and also how to accept forgiveness.

Integrity and humility should characterize relationships, but they must be perceived to be believed. This is an important distinction. One may have both integrity and humility, but if these traits are not clearly manifested, they are not perceived correctly. Sometimes missionaries will say "Well, you know I tried to do what was right, but it wasn't perceived that way."

Perseverance is an invaluable principle and must be a two-way process.

The last point here is that we must have an attitude of trying to understand the worldviews of the other partners. An illustration from Africa is a good example. Someone borrowed a watch from a friend of mine working on that continent. Years later, he got his watch back. It simply was not appropriate in that culture to go and ask for it to be returned. As long as the other person had a need for it, he was entitled to use it. That is part of a worldview.

Principles

Structures must be flexible, built on relationships. Consensus and contract are interrelated, but the emphasis is on consensus. What is put down in writing is not nearly as important as the consensus and the commitment to it.

Some mission agencies have had verbal agreements which worked. Others stress that it is important to have something in writing. One leader said, "In my early days, I wrote long, extended contractual agreements. And I had everything nailed down. But now I don't see that as all that invaluable any more."

Parameters are also necessary. One cannot simply say, "Well, let's just cooperate. Later, we will worry about how it works." Some parameters are needed for success.

Accountability is an important principle. Accountability depends upon shared vision, shared goals, shared methods, and an agreement on the basis of evaluation. Partnership members have to work at accountability, and it may be the weakest part of the partnership process in today's environment. In the area of accountability, the question is "How do we hold each other accountable?" Consensus would be primary; written agreements secondary.

Models

A tremendous opportunity exists for case studies. Some members of our group have done case studies in partnering, and we encourage those who have done so, to get that history together and make it available to the larger missions community. Models are often transferred without intention and need to be carefully thought through. How effectively has this been done? What has been learned? More case studies need to be circulating. Perhaps such reports could be included in the *Evangelical Missions Quarterly* or other publications in the future.

Types of Partnership

Types of partnership were explored in the mission-to-mission context. Most of this discussion focused on North American partnering. A lot of partnershipping in that framework is through multi-agency structures — partnershipping being done by organizations that work through a multitude of other relationships.

Two that come to mind quickly are InterServe and World Evangelical Fellowship — both multi-agency type partnerships. Other examples would be COMIBAM, which links together various missionary efforts in the region of Latin America; Indian Evangelical Mission, which would be similar to an interchurch type of partnership; and Partners International, who works with some seventy different partnership relationships.

A distinction was made between four types of partnership. One is the process that happens when two organizations merge together. Several members of the group had actually gone through the process of merging two mission agencies together, so it does happen. One of the main items for consideration is the philosophy of each group merging. The ethos and values of each cannot be ignored.

The second type is an adoption process where someone adopts another agency and endeavors to support it. There are a number of examples with Interdev being one of those. They do not have an agency focus; they have an adopted focus. Key items to be negotiated in this process include the "flagpole" issue (whose flag flies on top?), the funding issue (including ministry priorities and donor interest), and compatibility issues.

The third type occurs where a commitment is made to work together, but there is no formal agreement. This effort may be centered around a crusade and many times is project oriented. Key concerns center around strategy for the project.

The last type is a parenting relationship where one group actually brings into being another mission. This process brings up all the interesting challenges of parenting and even grandparenting. Key considerations would be stewardship responsibilities, leadership capabilities, organizational skills, and the process of "letting go" (the "apron string" syndrome).

A diagram was used showing the process of partnershipping. Starting with intent or desire for partnership, the process moves from there to cooperation to actual partnership to merger.

Intent -> Cooperation -> Partnership -> Merger

Four key steps were identified in that process:
1. Praying together; that includes developing a common vision, a sense of God's call, and the leading of the Holy Spirit.
2. Planning together; sitting down and talking it through.
3. Sharing personnel; the stress is on people before resources.
4. Sharing financially. Everybody woke up when we started talking about this one. The consensus is that resources are available to get the job done. One problem is the matter of designated versus undesignated giving. And much work needs to be done in thinking creatively about the transfer of funds from country to country.

In conclusion, several general rules are recommended:
1. Never do anything with money that will weaken the church.
2. Give financially to the organization, not to individual persons.
3. Do not support those areas that the church itself should do; i.e., support of national pastors.

4. Do not "skim off the cream" — take the best leaders away from the national church.

Section 5

❖❖❖

Two-Thirds World Partnerships

CHAPTER 13

Principles of Two-Thirds World Mission Partnership

Myung Hyuk Kim

Abstract: *A focus on mission partnership mainly in Asia and Korea. This presentation summarizes some major issues in partnership in missions and makes several proposals concerning partnershipping in Asian missions.*

A Story of Partnership

On April 29, 1991, the Korean women's ping-pong team defeated the unbeaten Chinese team and won the gold medal. For the first time in the history of a divided Korea, teams from the North and the South had combined in a single team to play at the forty-first international table tennis tournament held in Japan.

North and South Korea have been divided for the past 46 years. During the last 20 years, the North and the South Korean ping-pong teams had played in various international tournaments against each other about 145 times, but this was the first time they had formed a partnership. For the Korean people of both the North and the South this was a dramatic and moving event, not only because Korea won the gold medal, but mainly because it was won through a partnership between the North and the South.

There were some moving stories behind this partnership. During the first few days of some 30 days practice, the players of both teams felt uneasy with each other. They tried their utmost, however, to overcome the differences of dialect, attitude, and behavior. Both sides willingly accepted and used the dialect of the other side. Former first-string players who now had to become backup players were more than willing to sacrifice themselves and become merely practice mates for their team. After they won the gold medal, players from both teams expressed the fact that they would never want to be divided again.

This is more than an exciting story. It is a genuine challenge to the Korean Church which has not yet wholly united for partnership.

Introduction

My focus on partnership is mainly in relation to the situation in Asia and Korea. In the first part I will summarize some major issues in cooperation and partnership in missions. In the second section I present some proposals concerning principles of partnership in missions in Asia. Appendix B in the back of this volume contains interviews and questionnaires with a number of Asian missions leaders describing current situations of partnership in Asian missions.

Cooperation and Partnership in Missions— a Korean Case

Partnership, a biblical model

Man was created to live in fellowship with God and in partnership with his fellowmen. God, the creator, made Adam and Eve as partners. When Jesus sent out his disciples to be evangelists and missionaries, he sent them out two by two.

The Antioch Church followed this model when they sent out Paul and Barnabas as their missionaries. Paul maintained this basic principle of partnership and cooperation in missions for the rest of his life. He maintained partnership relationships with his mother church in Antioch as well as his daughter churches in Asia Minor and Europe. The Philippian Church became one of the best models of partnership in missions. Partnership was God's intention for man's life and work.

Partnership, a Korean model

Partnership manifested through Christian integrity. The Revs. Horace G. Underwood and Henry G. Appenzeller were two of the most successful Western missionaries to Korea in the beginnings of the Korean Church. They displayed a great example of partnership in missions. Underwood was a Presbyterian; Appenzeller a Methodist. Both came to Korea, arriving April 5, 1885, on the west coast of In-chon harbor on the same boat. When they were about to land, each insisted, according to an unidentified source, that the other party set foot on land first.

Partnership manifested through the policy of comity. This spirit of partnership and cooperation continued to be manifested among the missionaries. In 1892, when the Southern Presbyterians established their mission in Korea, the feeling was mutual that they should avoid duplication of labor and overlapping territories. In 1893 "the Council of Missions Holding the Presbyterian Form of Government" was organized, and the object of the body was "to carry on all our native work with a view to the organization of but one native Presbyterian Church in Korea."

At the first meeting of the Council in 1893, the Northern and Southern Presbyterians entered into agreement whereby the Southern Church was to occupy the two unoccupied southern provinces of Choong Chong and Cholla, and the Northern Church was to remain in the other parts of the country where they had already established themselves. Various missionaries were, however, soon confronted with territorial difficulties.

In order to prevent friction and overlapping in missions, in 1893 the Northern Presbyterians and Northern Methodists also entered into an agreement. The general principles established were that open ports and towns having a population of five thousand could be occupied by both missions; that smaller towns should be assigned to the first mission which established a substation there; and that no membership should be transferred without a letter of recommendation. The principle, generally known as the "principle of comity," gradually became the practical policy of missions until a rigid division of territory was made.

In 1905 the General Council of Protestant Evangelical Missions in Korea was formed with four Presbyterian missions and two Methodist missions. The purpose of the General Council was "to attempt cooperation in missions and as a result to organize one evangelical church in Korea." That purpose, however, was not realized.

Nevertheless the General Council contributed greatly in producing various united ministries in missions such as Bible translation, publishing literature, and publishing a union hymnal. Medical, educational, and Sunday School projects were cooperatively implemented.

Partnership integrated through the great revival of 1907. The great Korean revival of 1907 had a number of significant influences on the Korean Church. Among them was a removal of hidden conflict between missionaries and the Korean Church leaders, and an increase of mutual understanding and cooperation between them. The Western missionaries had had an attitude of superiority towards the Korean people. Koreans, on the other hand, had tended to follow the Western missionaries uncritically. Through the revival, however, both parties confessed to being sinners full of flaws and came to accept the others as partners.

Discord, a biblical example

Partnership and harmony were divine intentions for human life. Through sin, however, human beings were brought into discord and disharmony. Cain was angry with his brother Abel and killed him. Even the Apostle Paul had a sharp disagreement with Barnabas, his coworker in missions, and they separated from each other. Disputes cropped up among the Hellenist and Hebrew believers of the mother church in Jerusalem, among the believers at Corinth, and even among the faithful laborers at the Philippian Church.

Discord, a Korean example

The early missionary work in Korea was extremely successful in the light of the many political-cultural limitations. Yet, enduring problems of personal discord and disharmony among the Western missionaries were revealed. Disagreements arose between medical doctors Horace Allen and J. W. Heron (and Underwood). Dr. Allen wrote, "We have had a most surprising and provoking disagreement with Dr. Heron." Dr. Allen was close to the Korean government, and wanting to evade conflict with the government, tried to do indirect medical missions. Rev. Underwood as a Calvinistic Presbyterian missionary, however, wanted to do direct evangelistic and educational missions. Dr. Allen, as the senior member, tried to exert control.

Such disharmony among missionaries, however, did not create critical hindrances to early missions in Korea.

The Rev. Yang Sun Kim, a Korean Church historian, once pointed out that the Korean Church itself did not do well in practicing cooperation in the beginning of her history. "Most of the union ministry was done mainly through mutual cooperation by missions societies. Very little was done by the Korean Churches. The Korean Churches grew through the principle of self-support and self-propagation. Individual churches have grown greatly, yet little has been done for union ministry."

Competition and discord in missions in the modern Korean Church

Among the many problems the Korean Church has faced since the 1970s has been the spirit of competition and discord in missions.

Competitive individualism has been the most critical factor in the Korean Church's involvement in missions.

It is true, however, that the Korean Church has been reawakened to missions since the 1970s. David Dong Jin Cho, John Eui Whan Kim, and Chul Ha Han were among the missions leaders who challenged the Korean Church for missions. Many seminarians responded to the challenge and became pioneer missionaries of the second generation.

Competition and discord among the Korean Churches. Yet cooperation and partnership in missions were not always properly implemented among the Korean Churches. Cooperation between denominations and missions societies often did not happen, nor did missions leaders cooperate as they should. A strong denominationalism, individualism, and even an attitude of competitive heroism played greatly in missions. Missions were generally attempted separately; either individually, organizationally, or denominationally without any cooperation. The Korean Church could not cope with the newly arising missions movement, and denominations began to lose credibility.

Lack of cooperation between the Korean Church and the Western mission societies. In the 1970s, Western mission societies began to enter Korea. They easily drew the attention of Korean missionary candidates because they were experienced, well organized, and seemed credible. Many Korean missionary candidates went out to the mission fields through these agencies. And a number of Koreans went out to the fields through their own denominations.

Western mission societies certainly made positive contributions to the Korean Church. Missionary challenge, training, and placement all took place through them. Yet, the movement also had negative effects. The agencies made mission policies by themselves, without consultation with the Korean Church on such matters as recruiting, accepting, training, and placing. Legal and financial matters were also dealt with separately

Recently a few Korean branches of Western mission societies or West-based Korean mission societies have been organized. Some of these have tried to strengthen Korean voices. Cooperation however, has not yet been properly achieved. This may be because of the enduring conflict and tension between "modality" and "sodality," between Korean and Western behaviors, or between sect and group mindsets of the Korean Church leaders.

Discord among the Korean missionaries. Unfortunately, it is often pointed out that while one Korean missionary works well in the field, two of them cannot work together.

This saying has proven true in all too many cases. Inability to cooperate has become one of the most serious problems which Korean missionaries face. It may be because Korean people are monocultural and historically individualistic. Or it might be that the competitive self-centeredness of many Korean missionaries is something they have learned from their senior pastors in large churches in Korea. Some have even claimed that they were doing missions in a Korean style when they carried out mission tasks individualistically.

Lack of cooperation between the Korean Church and the field churches. Quite a few Korean missionaries were sent out to the fields without having an agreement with the field churches. When they are not supervised in the field, they are their own bosses and become a hindrance.

Voices of the Korean missionaries on partnership in missions

Recently I distributed a few questionnaires on partnership in missions to about one hundred Korean missionaries in the fields. The following is a summary of their responses.

Need of cooperation and partnership in missions. A majority of them expressed strong opinions about the fact that partnership is much needed for effective evangelism. Cooperation compensates for the weak aspects of Korean missionaries and eliminates unnecessary duplication of work and funding.

Problems of discord in the fields. Various problems of discord were pointed out. For instance, in the Philippines two theological seminaries were established in the same denomination and caused division.

In Brunei, cooperation with the Sarawak and Sabah natives was not well established because of the closed policy of the native churches. Recently interchange has occurred between the Brunei Church and the Korean Church, and as a result, more cooperation is being achieved.

In Thailand cooperation was not maintained because of mutual criticism and the spiritual immaturity of the Korean missionaries. In Japan missionaries have been competitive with each other, even making false reports back to the Korean Church. In Ecuador cooperation among ministers has not been well established because of differences in liturgy and life-style.

Problems arising from lack of cooperation. Lack of cooperation and discord among missionaries often provide heresies with opportunities to propagate and expand. The doors for evangelism become closed, and missionaries discredited. Unnecessary energy and money are wasted, and the effectiveness of missions is greatly lessened. Sometimes this even causes divisions in the field churches. God cannot get the glory through such actions.

Reasons for no cooperation. Self-centered heroism is the biggest reason for no cooperation. Competitive individualism, authoritarianism, superiority complexes, strong personalities, immature spirituality, lack of mutual understanding, denominationalism, nationalism, theological differences, no experience of cooperation at home, inadequate training for cross-cultural missions—these are all reasons given for no cooperation.

Mr. Eun Moo Lee, one of the pioneer Korean missionaries to Indonesia, once pointed out bluntly, "I found that the Korean type of individualism made it hard to cooperate with Western missionaries." Mr. Lee then stressed: "I believe that mutual understanding and mutual respect are the key factors to successful cooperation."

How to cooperate. Items that should be cultivated for cooperation in missions are: personal maturity, spiritual maturity, obtaining a right view of missions, practicing cooperation and interchange between churches and mission societies, receiving cross-cultural missions training, and overcoming individual church centeredness.

Present attempts at cooperation and partnership in missions

Formation of the Korea Partnership Missions Fellowship (KPMF). On January 18, 1988, the Korea Partnership Missions Fellowship was formed with missions leaders from six major evangelical Korean Churches (denominations) participating. The purpose of formation was to establish and maintain cooperation and partnership in missions. The purpose and rationale of the KPMF was stated as follows:

Now that the Korean Church has entered into her second century, she badly needs to establish a cooperative relationship among denominations, establish a partnership policy with the Western mission societies, and also carry out partnership agreements with the field churches.

Formation of the Korean World Mission Council. The formation of the Korean World Mission Council after the Korean World Mission '88 held at the Billy Graham Center, Wheaton, IL, July 25-30, 1988, was a great boost to create and encourage a spirit of partnership in missions among the Korean Churches in the U.S.A. Since the formation of the

Korean World Mission Council, the American Korean Churches have been actively and cooperatively engaged in world mission. The unity and cooperation of the Korean Churches have promoted missions in unprecedentedly significant ways.

Formation of the Korean World Missions Association (KWMA). On June 25, 1990, a more comprehensive missions association was formed at the Somang Presbyterian Church in Seoul. The initial organizing members of KWMA include church and missions leaders from a wider scope of denominations and missions societies. The KWMA was formed with the intention of merging with the KPMF.

Conclusion

Partnership is imperative for effective mission. Christ taught us in his Priestly Prayer in John 17 that sanctification and unity are the two prerequisites for mission. Jesus prayed to his Father to sanctify his disciples and to make them one so that the world might know and believe in Jesus Christ.

The Bible also teaches that God blesses those who are gathered and united to work together in His name. Therefore, we must strive and pray to establish partnership relationships between all missions-oriented persons and institutions. Churches and mission societies should cooperate; East and West should establish genuine partnerships; home and field must work together; and individuals, whether at home or on the field, should learn to cooperate.

Principles of Partnership in Missions in Asia

Why partnership?

The apostle Paul did not condemn divisive and competitive evangelism by some of his rivals. This was mainly because he was always happy whenever Christ was preached. At the same time, however, Paul kept exhorting believers and churches to be united in order to glorify God and make evangelism integral and credible. Jesus also exhorted his disciples and prayed for them that they might be one and united in order that they might glorify God and let the world know Him through them.

The basic and ultimate reason why we should cultivate cooperation and partnership is to glorify God and make evangelism integral. Of course churches can grow even when they are divided and competitive, as in the case of Korea. Some historians even justify divisive competition as one of the causes for church growth. This might be accepted when you look at the matter from a sociological standpoint. But from a spiritual standpoint, this cannot be justified. There is a saying that a sheet of paper is lighter when held by two persons. Even the Apostle Paul could not do missions alone. He was almost always assisted by helpers and was continuously related to and supported by home churches.

A single soldier is not able to fight all the hostile forces by himself. He needs support. The same is true with spiritual warfare. Partnership is imperative for effective mission. Quite a number of Korean missionaries have experienced disappointment or defeat in missions because they have not worked together. Duplication of ministry, waste of resources, confusion, and conflict often result from the lack of partnership.

What kinds of partnerships?

Partnership between church and society at home. Harmonious partnership was already established at the home church of Antioch before the first two missionaries were sent out. Different kinds of leaders at Antioch participated in prayers for, selection of, and the sending out of missionaries. Missions is a triune partnership ministry among God, missionary, and the church.

A missionary or a local church should establish partnership either with a denomination's missions committee or a mission society to do missions rightly. The denomination or the society should take responsibilities for providing missions information, holding missions seminars, recruiting and selecting missionary candidates, training the candidates, and placing the missionaries. The local churches should have responsibility for providing prayer and financial support.

Denominations should establish partnership with missions societies when they send out their missionaries through such societies. They should make an agreement on such matters as selecting, training, and placing missionaries, together with items involving the legal, financial, sabbatical, and retirement aspects of caring for the missionaries.

Two kinds of mistakes are being made, however. First, denominations tend to be autonomous and authoritative in carrying out missions.

Secondly, such traditional Western mission societies as OMF and Wycliffe insist on carrying out most of the policy making responsibilities by themselves while they take personnel and finances from Asian Churches. This is mainly because Western missions societies have a longer history, richer experience, and better structures. For the sake of effective mission, such Western dominance might be justified. Yet, if a new relationship of equal partnership between Asian churches and Western-based missions societies is not attempted, Asian churches will continue to remain unexperienced, ill-structured, and immature in missions.

Partnership with Western missions. I would like to propose an equal partnership relationship between Asian churches and Western-based mission societies as follows.

First, both parties should discuss together the first step of accepting missionary candidates. Some Western missions societies in Asia do not discuss this matter with the Asian churches. But the Asian churches bear the legal responsibilities for the missionaries such as applying for passports and visas.

Second, both parties should discuss finances. The Asian churches bear the financial responsibilities in such matters as fund-raising and sending funds. But some Western missions societies control the finances by themselves.

Third, such important policy making as placement and new programs of field ministry should be discussed by both parties, or at the very least reported.

Fourth, the "what" and "how" of ministry in the field should be committed into the hands of the field council of the missions society, for they are more experienced and knowledgeable about that field.

Fifth, the Asian Churches bear responsibilities for taking care of their missionaries on furloughs and retirement. These items should be discussed jointly.

Sixth, the Asian churches should invite experienced missions leaders from the West (on loan) to their own denomination's or association's missionary training programs to implement partnership missions.

Seventh, both parties should discuss together any problems on the field and try to solve them together.

As a reference I am including a sample of the agreement between the Korea Partnership Missions Fellowship (which will soon merge with the newly formed Korean World Missions Association) and WEC International.

1. The KPMF provides the evangelical Korean denominations and mission societies with information about WEC International and arranges for them to make agreements with WEC directly and to send their missionaries through WEC. Such an agreement between WEC and a denomination concerning an individual worker or couple will be similar to the following:

(a) The Korean denominations or mission societies will be responsible for the legal, financial, and administrative matters for the missionaries and their families whom they send. The Korean denominations or mission societies recognize these missionaries as belonging to the Korean denominations or mission societies on the field and directing the missionaries in their particular ministries. While these Korean missionaries belong to the Korean denominations or mission societies, they may also be regarded as members of WEC and ministers of the particular denominations on the field to which they are assigned.

(b) Important decisions such as the unsuitability of the candidate before placement, change of field or ministry, involvement in special missions projects, taking home leaves (furloughs) and disciplinary action should only be made in consultation with the Korean denominations or mission societies.

(c) This Agreement should be reviewed after four years and may be renewed after each term of service of each missionary through full consultation between the Korean denominations or mission societies, WEC, and the Korean missionaries:

(d) Termination of this agreement prior to the period specified in (d) above should only be considered after full discussions between the Korean denominations or mission societies, WEC, and the Korean missionaries. At least three months' notice of intended termination should be given.

2. The Agreement that KPMF and WEC makes does not preclude them from making further agreements with churches or missions that are not members of KPMF, though in prior consultation with KPMF.

3. This Agreement between KPMF and WEC should be reviewed after four years and may be renewed each four-year period.

4. Termination after this Agreement prior to the period specified in article three should only be considered after full discussions between KPMF and WEC. At least three months' notice of intended termination should be given.

Signed on 28 June 1989 by

Rev. Dr. Sun Hee Kwak, Chairman of the Korea Partnership Missions Fellowship

Rev. Dr. Myung Hyuk Kim, General Secretary of the KPMF

Dr. Dietrich Kuhl, International Secretary of WEC International

Mr. Colin Nicholas, British Director of WEC International

Partnership through a missions association. National churches together with national and international missions societies should develop a united partnership missions association. At present, missions associations in a number of Asian churches function merely as associations of fellowship. They just arrange missions seminars and some publications. Missions strategy and policy making are not yet discussed together.

In Korea, for example, an Association of Missions Societies has been formed. It, as a government registered body, has carried on the function of issuing recommendations of member societies to the government on legal matters. A more recently formed (January 18, 1988) association is the Korea Partnership Missions Fellowship (KPMF). Even though it has at least created a spirit of cooperation and opened the way towards a more positive partnership in missions in Korea, it has not done much except for holding a number of missions seminars and making agreements with such agencies as WEC, AIM, and IMF.

On June 25, 1990, another association of wider missions leadership in Korea was formed, called the Korean World Missions Association (KWMA). The initial organizing members include church and missions leaders of wider denominations and missions societies. The KWMA was formed with the intention of merging with the KPMF. Even though I am not yet optimistic about the future, I sincerely hope this could develop into a genuine missions association. The purpose of the KWMA was clearly stated in its preface as the following.

"In spite of spiritual growth, however, the Korean Church has been lacking in unity and mutual cooperation for effective missions. Hereby we establish the Korean World Missions Association in order to carry out missions through cooperation and partnership between the Church and the missions societies.

"The KWMA should function as a center to provide the whole body of the Korean Church with up-to-date missions information, to provide training programs with qualified missions specialists, to provide a forum to discuss and build missions strategies, to provide a place and system to educate missionary kids, and to provide even a place and system to take care of missionaries on furloughs and retirement.

"Initial responsibilities to build such a real partnership missions association rest upon the Korean churches which are willing to overcome self-centered and competitive heroism. A substantial encouragement and support, however, should come from the Western missions societies. West-based missions societies should encourage and help to develop Asia-based missions associations in each Asian country similar to their own missions societies by providing missions materials and by loaning missions specialists.

"The first meaningful project of the KWMA is to hold a missions conference to evangelize the nation and the world (looking towards AD 2000) in November, 1991, in Seoul, Korea. It will be sponsored by the Korean World Missions Association, the Korean World Missions Council in the U.S.A., and the Korean Christian Mission Center. The conference will be participated in by most of the Korean missions leaders, both in Korea and in the U.S.A., together with some field-experienced Korean missionaries to discuss and to build missions strategies to evangelize Korea and the world."

Partnership in the field. Missionaries should establish and maintain partnership relationships with field churches or field missions societies. The essential task of missionaries is to preach the gospel of Jesus Christ and to build native churches in the field. Missionaries are not supposed to build their own churches or denominations but are to build and strengthen native churches and denominations. This is why they should establish an assisting and partnership relationship with native churches or missions societies. Missionaries should not initiate any new missions project or ministry without consulting with national churches. Missionaries in the field could also establish and develop a partnership missions association in the field. The missions association in the field, consisting of individual missionaries and their missions branch, should provide them not only with opportunities for fellowship but with practical forums at which mission strategies as well as field problems and needs are discussed.

The Western missions societies could encourage and support such field missions associations. The missions association in the field could also help develop a place and system to educate missionary children.

Partnership among the field missionaries. Missionaries in the field could also arrange to hold missionary conferences among themselves regularly every few years to encourage and educate themselves. The Korean missionaries in the fields all around the world, for example, hold a missionary conference in a different place every three or four years. In 1991 it was held in Singapore.

Partnership among Asian churches and missions societies. It is the right time for Asian churches and Asian missions societies to establish cooperation in missions to face the challenge of independence and responsibility. The Asian Mission Association (AMA) has been a pioneer in this attempt, though it has been limited to coordinating missions forces in Asia. The AMC of 1990 was a great step in that direction. The Evangelical Fellowship of Asia (EFA) Missions Committee should function as a forum and channel by which partnership in missions can be encouraged and practiced.

How can we cooperate in partnership?

Equality. Partnership does not mean that each party should be equal in terms of ability or possession. It means that each party is given its own unique status and tasks. One talent and five talents are not equal from a human standpoint, but they can be regarded equal from God's point of view. Partnership, therefore, can be achieved only when each stands in the presence of God.

Humility. Discord and disharmony in missions do not usually arise from a lack of principles, but rather a lack of personal qualities. The most important ingredient of partnership is humility. The humility of servanthood was the quality which Jesus Christ himself manifested as the supreme model of a missionary. When Paul exhorted unity among believers he always stressed humility.

Arrogance, bitterness, and self-centered ambition will destroy partnership. But unselfish leadership with genuine humility is most needed in modern missions. This is given as a gift from God, and we need to pray for it. Give us the mind of Jesus Christ who said "I am gentle and humble in heart."

Conclusion

A spirit of cooperation and partnership is imperative for effective mission. Christ taught us in his Priestly Prayer in John 17 that sanctification and unity are the two prerequisites for missions. Jesus prayed to his Father to sanctify his disciples and to make them one so that the world might know and believe in Jesus Christ. God pronounces blessings upon brothers and sisters dwelling in unity and ministering in cooperation.

Another important thing we learn from the Scriptures is that a spirit of unity and cooperation is not anything which can be achieved by human goodness or efforts alone but rather is something which should be prayed for; something contrary to human nature, yet something which God provides as a blessing. That is why Jesus not only commanded but also prayed to his Father. "Father, make them one as we are one." Therefore, we must do our utmost and pray to establish cooperation and partnership relationships among all missions-oriented persons and institutions.

Churches and societies should cooperate. East and West as well as North and South should establish a real partnership relationship. Home and field must cooperate. Individuals, whether at home or on the field, should work together in unity. The basic obstacles to cooperation including competitive individualism, ambitious heroism, the mammoth church syndrome, British or Western imperialism, or exclusive Third-World nationalism should be overcome at all costs to obey the Great Commission of the Lord.

Another basic obstacle—the immature personality of missionaries—should be overcome by careful recruiting and intensified spiritual and cross-cultural community training. It is time to exchange information among Asian churches and locate needs and resources.

The kind of leadership we need today is that of the "unambitious" man of God. Only such persons, with the help of the transforming power of the Holy Spirit, can create the spirit of cooperation and partnership for missions among us.

O God, our Father and Lord of the harvest, raise up among us servant-leaders that they may encourage us to serve you in unity and cooperation to carry out the Great Commission which you have given us. Father, sanctify us and make us all one in Jesus Christ that the world might know Him and believe in Him. Amen.

Chapter 14

The Philippine Missions Association: A Case Study

Met Castillo

Abstract: *A description of the Philippine Missions Association (founded in 1983), a partnership of different missions bodies on the national level. PMA has 27 member groups and three types of membership: local church missions committees, denominational missions departments/committees, and independent mission agencies.*

Introduction

In Asia, we have a magic word. That word is "relational."

When partnerships are viewed from the relational aspect, one can work in some way with almost anybody. Our mission, for instance, had a Filipino missionary from a Pentecostal church, supported by some Baptist and evangelical churches, who worked with a Presbyterian church in Taiwan.

Partnership has been in the thinking of church and mission leaders for some time. But it seems that during these days a new focus on its meaning and practical implications to the worldwide missionary task of the Church is on the rise. As missions continue to emerge from the Two-Thirds world and objective self-examination becomes the experience of Western missions, the need for genuine partnership becomes the most urgent agendum of mission leaders. As Maurice Sinclair points out, "Partnership is not just a nice idea or fashionable style for doing missions. It is, from the Biblical standpoint, essential to mission itself" (*Ripening Harvest, Gathering Storm*, Bromley, Kent: MARC, 1988, 203).

Partnership in missions is essential to the missionary enterprise for several reasons. First, it is the highest form of *koinonia* in the New Testament. Koinonia in the NT has three basic meanings: fellowship, generosity, and participation or partnership. Koinonia as partnership is "having a share in something with someone." Koinonia in missions simply means having a share in the task of world evangelization with other mission groups.

The second reason has to do with the vastness of the remaining work to be done. No one mission group, or even an aggregation of mission agencies, has the full capability and resources to do a thorough job.

The third reason is closely related to the second. The urgency of the task requires that we put our efforts together. More can be accomplished in partnership than working alone.

Finally, missions in partnership serves as an eloquent witness to the unity of the church and the universality of the Gospel that Christians preach to the world.

Founding of Philippine Missions Association

For the above-mentioned reasons, the Philippine Missions Association (PMA) was established. As early as 1979, key leaders of the evangelical churches in the Philippines discussed the need of a national missions organization. But the fulfillment of this dream did not come about until four years later.

In 1983 a National Missions Consultation, participated in by the leaders of mission agencies and committees, gave a clear mandate to organize such a mission structure. On December 2, 1983, the Philippine Missions Association was formally inaugurated and gained its legal personality with the Philippine government as an umbrella organization for local church missions committees, denominational departments of missions, and independent mission agencies. To date there are 27 member groups. In this sense, PMA is basically a partnership of different missions bodies on the national level.

Purposes of PMA

The purposes of the PMA are to:
1) promote cooperative action in missionary endeavors
2) provide coordination service and missionary information among its members
3) assist churches in their missions programs
4) serve as a sending body when member groups are unable to discharge this function
5) act as a receiving agency for missionaries sent to the Philippines

Looking at the above purposes, PMA is unique in that it goes one step beyond a traditional mission agency. It is both a sending and receiving missions body. It sends out Filipino missionaries within and outside the Philippines and at the same time receives missionaries coming into the country, primarily those who are sent by other Asian mission organizations.

At the present time, PMA has three missionary families working among tribes in the northern Philippines and seven missionary personnel serving in Niger, Ethiopia, Bolivia, Chile, and Paraguay. The Association has received or sponsored missionaries from Indonesia, Korea, and Singapore under a special working agreement.

PMA is basically a partnership, not only on the national level, but also in working with regional and international missions. The remaining part of this paper will discuss these levels of partnership, but allow me to mention briefly at this juncture two practical problems, for which we attempt to provide adequate solutions through partnership with other missions.

These two problems which are unique in the Philippine context are government restrictions and the lack of mission funds. Since missions is still in its infancy insofar as the Philippine churches are concerned, PMA resorted to the pooling of resources in order to facilitate the sending of Filipino missionaries.

The church in the Philippines is blessed with rapid growth. More than 23,000 local churches dot the towns, cities, and villages. Half of these were established during the immediate past decade. Through the Discipling A National Movement (DAWN 2000), many more churches are being planted. We have a goal of 50,000 churches by 2000 A.D. Most of the churches are economically poor. However, being poor is no excuse for not doing missions. Limited funds can be utilized with maximum results by working together in partnership.

In addition to the problem of meager funds, government financial restrictions make it difficult for us to send missionary support to other countries. Due to prevailing economic conditions in the country, the government prohibits the remittance of foreign exchange outside the country. It seems that the Lord has gifted the churches in the Philippines with ready missionary personnel, but due to these two problems mission sending is somewhat hampered.

In the mind of the leaders and members of PMA, such difficulties are not insurmountable. In fact, these problems, coupled with the burden of reaching the hitherto unreached peoples, prompted us to seek some form of partnership with other groups.

Partnership Among Local Missions

PMA has three types of membership: local church missions committees, denominational missions departments/committees, and independent mission agencies. To date, there are 27 member groups and a good number of these are sending missions themselves. Most of these sending missions send their missionaries in cooperation with their founding missions or churches. Such is the case of the Christian and Missionary Alliance Churches in the Philippines, the Church of the Foursquare, Association of Bible Churches which works very closely with Send International, the Philippine Home Council of the Overseas Missionary Fellowship, and others.

The type of partnership on the national or local level is largely networking and providing assistance in recruitment, training, support raising, and placement. PMA serves as the monitoring agency as well as the resource center for its own members. A classic example is the case of a missionary candidate from the mission department of the Association of Bible Churches, who applied to the Philippine Council of OMF and was endorsed to serve as a missionary under OM Philippines.

In the area of mission support, I mentioned the Filipino missionary from a Pentecostal church who worked with a Presbyterian church in Taiwan. We exchange personnel and we share the burden of support and a common goal of reaching the unreached.

Partnership with Regional Missions

Partnership with Indonesia Missionary Fellowship (IMF)

"The IMF and PMA seek to establish a partner mission relationship to work together in cross-cultural ministry, to achieve mutual goals in evangelism, church planting, leadership, and supportive ministries to the glory of God...." Thus begins the working agreement (WA) which was signed on March 2, 1986.

For several years, IMF prayed to send missionaries to the Muslim people. They finally made it to Surinam and Pakistan, but their missionary to Pakistan returned home after six months for lack of visa. They then turned their eyes to other countries in Asia. In 1984 I was privileged to minister among the students of the IMF Bible Institute and young people in Batu Malang, East Java. I presented the need to experiment on another approach to Muslim evangelism in the Philippines and challenged the Indonesian Churches to respond by sending their missionaries to the islands of Mindanao and Sulu where Muslim Filipinos reside.

This new approach would involve Asian missionaries who are either converts or from Muslim background. IMF responded very positively and on March 4, 1987, the first Indonesian couple arrived on location in Mindanao. Two years later another Indonesian couple arrived on the field. Both couples are performing excellently in reaching the Tausog Muslims in Zamboanga peninsula.

PMA's partnership with IMF is a two-way approach. IMF sends missionaries to the Filipino Muslims, and their missionaries come under the official sponsorship and administration of PMA. But their support is solely the responsibility of IMF. PMA also can send missionaries to Indonesia to work with IMF, but due to lack of support, this is not yet in operation.

As mentioned earlier, the partnership relationship is governed by a written working agreement duly signed by the leaders of each group. Some pertinent provisions of the agreement are as follows:

1) The missionary has dual membership status with both IMF and PMA.

2) The appointment of the missionary is subject to the approval of both agencies in accordance with the standards established by each agency.

3) PMA supervises the securing of visas and makes other arrangements necessary for the beginning of field work.

4) IMF is responsible for the financial and prayer support of the missionary.

5) PMA directs the activities of the missionary on the field and provides financial supervision.

6) While on the field, the missionary comes under the supervision of the General Secretary of PMA; while on furlough he comes under the responsibility of IMF.

7) Progress reports and information during furlough will be provided by IMF to PMA.

8) The missionary shall not solicit for personal funds from home or field constituencies of either agency without prior permission of the respective agency.

The experiment seems to be working very well. The missionaries have not only learned the language (Tausog), but they have also adjusted easily to the Tausog culture. Consequently, they are well received by the Tausogs and are greatly used in evangelism and church planting. In view of this initial success, PMA has made further request for additional Indonesian missionaries to work among another language group in Muslimland.

Partnership with Korea International Mission (KIM)

The second partnership on the regional level that PMA has entered into is with Korea International Mission (KIM), Seoul, South Korea. KIM is one of the large mission groups in the region and has missionaries in many parts of the world. In 1988, KIM saw the need to expand its field to the Philippines, and after a series of meetings the leaders of KIM and PMA agreed to work in partnership.

This partnership is similar to the partnership with IMF. The salient point on the "Cooperative Agreement Between KIM and PMA" has to do with missionary sending from Korea to the Philippines. PMA serves as the official sponsor and supervisor of KIM missionaries. KIM, on the other hand, recruits and assigns the missionary and raises his or her support.

The "Cooperative Agreement" was signed by KIM on October 4, 1988, and by the General Secretary of PMA on September 26 of the same year. On November 23, 1988, the first missionary couple arrived in Manila. This couple with two young boys has been given three primary areas of ministry:

1) Teach missions in any Bible School endorsed by PMA
2) Initiate a research project for the unreached peoples of the Philippines
3) Assist PMA General Secretary in promoting missions nationwide

The KIM-PMA partnership is currently being expanded beyond the sponsorship of missionary personnel. Very recently, KIM took a step further by organizing its own mission structure in the Philippines, called KIM Philippines. Since this move was done without prior consultation with PMA, it could be a potential cause of irritant in the existing relationship. It could eventually render the current "Cooperative Agreement" unnecessary inasmuch as KIM-Philippines could take care of the function of providing legal and administrative sponsorship for their own missionaries.

KIM-Philippines has expressed the desire to apply as a member of the PMA, but nothing has been formalized. Suffice it to say at this point that the current PMA-KIM partnership stands in need of further study and consequent revision to insure smooth relationship.

Partnership with Faith Mission Church (FMC)

Partnership with Faith Mission Church is unique in the sense that the relationship is with a local church rather than a mission agency. FMC is a relatively young church, but it has a keen interest in missions as shown in its name. In fact, it was established with a missions-focused purpose. They wanted to send their own missionary, but being small and lacking in experience they opted to seek partnership with PMA, which would serve as the receiving and sponsoring agency for their own missionary.

A "Partner Mission Agreement" between FMC and PMA, the content of which is generally similar with the "Agreements" mentioned earlier, was signed by the pastor of the church on June 3, 1987, and by the general secretary of PMA on September 4, 1987.

FMC's first missionary couple arrived in the Philippines in 1987 and after language study (Tagalog), they were assigned to work with a member mission of PMA. They were given a two-pronged ministry, namely to teach in a Bible school located in the province of Nueva Ecija and to reach international students who are studying in a nearby agricultural university. This is probably one of the most meaningful missionary assignments in the history of PMA. We could also say the same thing about the existing partnership relationship between FMC and PMA.

As in the partnerships mentioned earlier, FMC recruits, sends, and supports its own missionary. PMA, on the other hand, serves as official sponsor or receiving body and in consultation with FMC and the missionary himself, determines the assignment and provides supervision. While on the field the missionary is responsible to the General Secretary of PMA, and while on furlough or on leave, comes directly under the responsibility of FMC.

FMC has sent a second couple to the Philippines. Because of its deep conviction on thorough missionary preparation, this couple, like the first, completed Bible College education in Singapore. But before they went to Singapore Bible College, this couple spent a term in Nigeria. Now they are serving in the Philippines doing evangelism among the urban poor in Manila. .

Partnership with International Missions

In terms of time sequence, PMA's partnership with SIM East Asia, which is one of the Councils of SIM International, came first before its partnership with regional missions (Asia). The "Partner Mission Agreement," which became the basis of other working agreements, was signed by the General Secretaries of both agencies on March 1, 1985, and revised on October 5, 1990 (see Appendix D).

The role of PMA in its regional partnership is mainly receiving or sponsoring missionaries from other Asian countries. In its agreement with SIM East Asia, with an office in Singapore, PMA fulfills its role as a sending mission. It recruits and trains its own missionaries and then sends them to the mission fields through SIM. Under this arrangement, PMA has sent five missionary units to Africa and Latin America (two families and three singles) between 1986 to 1990, or an average of one missionary unit each year. Lord willing, we want to keep the record and at present we have two units who are preparing to go plus more than a dozen applicants.

As in the other agreements, missionaries have dual membership. Once accepted and located on the field, they come under the supervision of SIM. Before that and during furlough, they are responsible to PMA. Choosing the field of assignment is primarily the duty of SIM, which also determines the field budget of the missionary. But PMA determines the outgoing budget.

The provision of the Agreement affecting finances is different from the other arrangements, and this factor does assist PMA in confronting the two practical problems of inadequate funds and governmental restrictions. The agreement provides that, in cooperation with the Filipino missionary and his home church, PMA is responsible to raise the outgoing expense budget (OE) which includes airfares, travel documents, promotion, and deputation. SIM is responsible to raise the field budget of the missionary from individuals and churches in Asia and other countries. PMA also assists SIM whenever possible.

However, the foregoing picture is undergoing minor modification. In the revised Agreement, PMA's share in the missionary's expenses has been increased beyond the OE. Filipino missionaries are now to raise support from whatever sources available to them and by looking to God to supply all their needs. This means that they are to raise support from the Philippines also, and support raised in the Philippines shall be kept for outgoing, furlough, return ticket, administration, retirement benefits, and deputation ministry. Since these funds do not get out of the country, any government restriction does not apply on them.

The PMA-SIM partnership is working very well so far. It is fair, built on mutual respect, and is a real help in mobilizing Filipino missionaries. This relationship provides specific solutions to our problems and is a growing partnership. However, it is not the only way through which PMA sends forth its missionaries. We will continue to send through SIM, but at the same time we will seek other means, whether through new partnerships or direct sending.

Conclusion

I will conclude this simple case study of an emerging mission in the Philippines by making a list of observations and general statements.

1) PMA was born out of a strong desire on the part of the church leaders in the Philippines to develop a missions movement responsive to the needs and challenges of the times.

2) It was originally conceived on the principle of Christian partnership among missions organizations on the local and national level. Later, PMA entered into partnership with missions organizations in Asia or on a regional level, and on the international level as well, because of its deep desire to mobilize Filipino missionaries whose number is growing rapidly. It also had a strong desire to get involved in world evangelization, especially among the hitherto unreached peoples.

3) Such partnership on three levels is relatively young, and it offers itself to objective evaluation to insure its healthy growth and development.

4) Recognizing the wealth of personnel resources in the churches, and at the same time the limited financial resources, PMA continues to seek other viable means of facilitating the sending of Filipino missionaries. We have initiated discussion with certain groups about tentmakers, whom I prefer to call vocational missionaries. This is one way of moving our missionaries to the field of service, but it will be limited and will mobilize a special type of missionary personnel. We therefore need to look into other means of partnership.

5) Finally, PMA wants to explore certain specific possibilities of helping reach the unreached peoples which are mostly in Asia. We want to send Filipino missionaries to them, but we also want to keep the door open for other missionaries to come and help us reach the unreached peoples groups in the Philippines.

(For further information on the modern Philippine missionary movement, see the interview with Met Castillo in Appendix C.)

CHAPTER 15

Two-Thirds World Group Report

Facilitator: Larry Pate

Abstract: *From the perspective of partnerships in the Two-Thirds world, this group report addresses basic issues including characteristics and dangers of partnership agreements and readiness factors in seeking relationships. Three action steps with proposals are recommended.*

Introduction

The Working Group for Two-Thirds world mission partnerships discussed a number of questions related primarily to partnerships between Two-Thirds world churches and agencies on local, regional, and international levels. Those questions and the points of consensus are listed below. In the concluding section, three action steps containing proposals are suggested.

Discussion Questions

QUESTION: **What are the characteristics of effective partnership agreements?**

1. Flexibility in terms of organizational policy and structure
2. Responsiveness to change
3. Characterized by mutual respect and trust
4. A strategic fit between the partnering groups which facilitates the achivement of partnership goals
5. Equality—harmonious service for the task while retaining diversity of partnership members
6. Strong commitment to common goals
7. An adequate level of compatibility in missions theology
8. Adequate, open communication and strong interpersonal ties between leaders

9. Adequate commitment to the process of developing the partnership.

10. Created, led, and directed by the Spirit of God

QUESTION: What are the dangers to be guarded against in establishing missions partnerships?

1. Paternalistic attitudes must be avoided.

2. Avoid unrealistic expectations in the partnership development process. People are surprised at the amount of energy and time necessary to establish and develop a partnership. Some people frankly said that if they had known what it took, they would have been slower in entering into it. Secondly, they said they would have probably tried to find projects to partner on which were more significant so that the process of development would be more worthwhile in the long run.

3. Seek to insure that the products of partnership, rather than the partnership itself, remain the focus. This does not diminish the value of the process of developing the relationships. It is just a recognition that sometimes partnership can become an end in itself if not watched carefully.

4. Avoid developing syndromes of dependency. A number of Asians pointed out that just as there are cultural imperialistic tendencies in the Western missions movement, there can also be the same thing in the non-Western missions movement.

5. Guard against a domineering spirit and encourage creative approaches. Some monolithic, hierarchical church leadership structures have developed in portions of the world where the church grows rapidly. This may tend toward a domineering attitude by the leadership. If they do not have a vision for missions, this can have a stifling effect on the development of partnerships and missions in general — not only international partnerships but even partnerships within local countries, and perhaps especially in those, because there is a certain unhealthy competition that develops in that kind of context.

QUESTION: What vital missionary tasks and activities have yet to be accomplished because partnership is required for the successful completion?

The thought behind this question is, "What has never been dreamed or tried or thought seriously about because the kind of partnership that would be required is so much out of the norm that nobody ever considered it?" At least five points were raised — not exhaustive but significant:

1. Needs related to Two-Thirds world missionaries.
* Education of missionary children
* Pension plans, medical care, insurance
* Other culture-specific reentry needs
* Pastoral care of the missionary family

A vital area for the Two-Thirds world is the education of missionary children. This issue was solved to some degree, in the Western missions movement, over a period of two hundred years. Western missionaries' children generally are able to return home, fit back into their culture, and succeed — perhaps even excel.

But that is not the case in the majority of the non-Western missionary movement and particularly in cultures which are most non-Western — Asian cultures, for instance. When these children are not only coming back into an educational system, but also a job market peculiar to their own society, they may be perceived as tainted in their own culture. A daughter may not even be marriageable.

Missionary care needs have also been much neglected in many parts of the non-Western missions movement, though not all. How do missionaries survive when they become too old to care for themselves?

In addition, pastoral care of the missionary family is an issue of increasing importance in most portions of the missions movements which are still in their earlier stages — Latin America, for instance. It is difficult for Latin American missions to provide the totality of pastoral care needed for their missionaries.

2. Creative-access target areas can be more easily tackled by Two-Thirds world missions willing to work in partnership.

3. Intercontinental projects and networking. A lot could be done between continents and regions which has not been attempted yet because partnership was not advanced enough in the larger missionary movement. The potential for this happening seems good, partially because of matters which developed between delegates at the Consultation.

4. Local, regional, and international research projects — plus dissemination of the information — can and should be initiated and coordinated by partnerships within the Two-Thirds world missions community.

There was a strong level of consensus that within the Two-Thirds world, research has to come on line as one of the priorities. Goals need to be set and sold in the churches so that they own those goals. Then, wherever the resources come from, the plan is still a localized, nationalized, non-Western piece of missionary agenda.

5. Networks and systems with non-traditional resource development can be stimulated and reproduced through Two-Thirds world mission partnerships. In India, it is likely that a law will be instituted to the effect that no outside funding will be allowed into India for the purposes of spreading and propagating religion. Therefore a lot of the partnerships that have already developed between the West and the mission agencies in India could easily be cut off. There is a growing feeling that God has resources out there in the non-Western world which have not been tapped for mission effectively. They need some partnering to tap and train those resources, to motivate them, to give them the vision.

QUESTION: What are the factors that help determine readiness for seeking partnership relationships?

Here are some of the factors that seem related to the development of partnership:

—The context of the target people
—The resources of the churches in the partnering countries
—The amount of resources in the target area
—The level of responsiveness to the gospel in the target region
—The amount of experience in partnership

Some of the relationships between the above factors can be depicted by the following model. There are certain contexts, both national and regional, in which there may be high resources or low resources, a low response to the gospel or a high response to the gospel, and where there is a relationship between those in terms of the tendency toward partnership. That relationship is shown through this matrix.

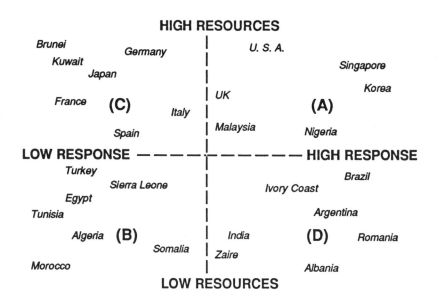

HIGH RESOURCES

Brunei
          Germany   U. S. A.
  Kuwait
         Japan   Singapore
                                       Korea
  France **(C)**   UK   **(A)**
             Italy
     Spain   Malaysia   Nigeria

LOW RESPONSE — — — — | — — — — — **HIGH RESPONSE**

  Turkey   Brazil
        Sierra Leone   Ivory Coast
   Egypt
Tunisia   Argentina
   Algeria **(B)**   India   **(D)** Romania
         Somalia   Zaire
Morocco   Albania

LOW RESOURCES

In target regions where resources of all types are low, outside partnership is a practical necessity. So in the lower left quadrant, these people are faced with an absolute necessity for partnership in order to see the gospel spread. They have a high motivation toward partnership.

On the other hand, in countries and regions of high resources, partnership tends to be viewed more as an option but not a necessity. This trend is in the process of being overcome in many parts of the world, as the church increasingly identifies itself globally.

But a combination of low response and limited resources are clear signs of the need for partnership. So churches in regions where the church enjoys high resources and/or high response should set as priorities partnerships with churches in low response/low resource areas.

Spiritual capital is as important as financial capital in assessing potential for partnership development. In other words, one group can have a tremendous potential for partnership in a high response area even though it may not have high resources for a number of reasons.

There are a lot of things people in the lower right quadrant cannot do without partnership. But their advantage is that they have a lot more believers— they have a larger portion of the Body of Christ. God did not say one has to be rich to have partnership. Neither did He say one has to be rich to go to the mission field. These two parts need to work together.

It is interesting how these people, when they think of mission in the high-response but low-resource areas, automatically think of partnership. This is what Two-Thirds world brothers and sisters would have us understand — some leadership for partnership is developing from within the Two-Thirds world that could lead the Western world. Models showing that taking place already to some degree were present at the Consultation.

Action Steps With Proposals

Keep in mind that these action steps are mostly from the minds of Two-Thirds world missions leaders. These were not necessarily Western leaders putting these action steps together. These are very much on the top of the agenda for Two-Thirds world missions.

1. Non-Western missionary movements often stand in danger of being paralyzed by missionary attrition resulting from non-existing or insufficient education for missionary children. If MK's cannot receive education on the field which prepares them adequately for reentry into their own culture, missionaries cannot remain on the field.

> **Proposal:** Let there be a call for national level consultations in the Two-Thirds world to address the problems in each context. Let there also be regional and international consultations to stimulate partnership and understanding in the worldwide missions community.

2. There is too wide a disparity between missionary training available in the Two-Thirds world. There must be greater cooperation and partnership within various regions and internationally to more effectively distribute training personnel and resources. While there are tremendous models of missionary training developing in the Two-Thirds world, they are often congregated in certain regions quite heavily, and almost nonexistent in other areas. The idea is to network to get training resources disseminated more strategically within the Two-Thirds world missions movement.

> **Proposal:** Let there be more Two-Thirds world involvement in cooperative efforts in missionary training. Let regional and international consultations and training networks be encouraged and prioritized.

3. There is a quantum growth in the need for funding Two-Thirds world missions, together with increasing nationalistic restrictions on receiving such funding from international sources. There are growing pressures to generate local funding for Two-Thirds world missions.

> **Proposal:** Let there be a new type of international network developed which brings together Christian entrepreneurs interested in generating resources for the Two-Thirds world missions.

The financial needs of Two-Thirds world missions are growing rapidly because their missions are growing so fast. When the need for funding Two-Thirds world missions is considered together with the potential for government restrictions on the receipt of international funds in certain regions of the world, there will be an even greater shortage of funds available. Thus, it becomes obvious that there needs to be some sort of concerted effort to generate funds from within the Two-Thirds world context wherever they are sending their own missionaries.

The feeling was expressed concerning the North American context that a lot of money is available but mischanneled. At least, a lot of Christian money gets mischanneled because the Christian entrepreneur or wealthy person tends to get disconnected from the local church or missions projects and winds up more in the philanthropic milieu of society at large—giving to universities, hospitals, and organizations of that type. But some of the Two-Thirds world leaders expressed the feeling that the same is often true in their countries. Somehow a dichotomy has existed in too many parts of the world between God's people and God's money.

The members of our group found it stimulating to be with so many people from different cultures, representing many different parts of the world. We were forced, not only to recognize various agendas of the missions movements in different parts of the world, but also to recognize the need for cooperation in all these agendas.

Section 6

❖❖❖

Conclusion

CHAPTER 16

Partnerships: Path to the Future

Larry D. Pate

Abstract: *A rising interest in partnership efforts is a healthy indication that the evangelical church is becoming serious about accomplishing the remaining tasks of world evangelization. A summary of the Working Consultation on Partnership is given, emphasizing two major contributions: the concept of "horizontal-vertical integration" and a graphic matrix which illustrates the difficulties and opportunities related to partnership development and how they are affected by the economic and spiritual context.*

Introduction

Computer arch-rivals IBM Corporation and Apple end years of bitter rivalry to form a technological alliance.

Two of the West's most powerful banking competitors merge.

In bold headlines, the front page of the *Chicago Tribune* (July 6, 1992) proclaims a meeting of the "Group of Seven." Leaders of seven of the world's major economic powers (United States, Japan, Germany, France, Great Britain, Italy, and Canada) are beginning talks in Munich. Highlighting their agenda are such international topics as Yugoslavian violence, revamping of the world's outdated trading system, safety improvements of nuclear reactors in Eastern Europe, and the ailing economies of the former Soviet republics. Russian President Boris Yeltsin appeals to these G-7 leaders for a $24 million aid package from the International Monetary Fund.

Such cooperative efforts color the news media on a daily basis. "Partnership" is a generic term we might use to describe the growing number of these political and/or economic strategic alliances.

We have entered a period of rapid political, economic, social, and religious change. At first glance, the cause of the change may appear to be political developments in the "second world" Communist nations.

With the failure of much Communist ideology, the "Third world," long accustomed to playing off "First" and "Second" worlds against each other and financing their countries in the process, now realize that the playing field on which nations must compete has changed drastically. From Albania to Zaire, nations of the non-Western world are positioning themselves to compete in a global marketplace under comparatively lassez-faire capitalist rules. Leaders in politics, business, and religion are scrambling to take advantage of such rapid and dramatic changes.

In this period of rapid transition, we should understand, however, that the root cause is not political, but rather technological. The collapse of Communist ideology, whatever the weaknesses of the system, was precipitated by sweeping technological changes impacting every sphere of human life.

Information Technology: the Engine of Change

Leaders in every sphere tend to look at symptoms in their field and pronounce them causes. Political leaders point to the collapse of Communist ideology as the root cause of current changes. Sociologists tend to view such changes as the result of global urbanization. Religious leaders describe them in prophetic terms.

There is doubtless some truth in these claims, but if futurologists such as Alvin Toffler, John Naisbitt, and George Gilder are correct, the underlying cause for these momentous changes lies in the transition from an industrial to an information driven age. *The dawning of the information age is the underlying fundamental reason global change is accelerating in every major arena of human endeavor.*

Consider a few facts and projections:

-> 52% of the U. S. gross national product is spent in the communications industries.

-> 60% of all jobs are in communications-related fields.[1]

-> By the year 2000, a large percentage of managerial decisions will be based upon computer "expert systems" which will gather data electronically and issue reports automatically, recommending actions according to data untouched by human hands.

-> By the year 2000, large reference works and library card catalogs will be more economically produced and available on compact disk media than on print media. This will enable a quantum leap in research quality and advance man's knowledge at an accelerating rate.[2]

The Globalization of Missions

Technology is making the world a different place. Information-age changes occurring in various spheres will have an increasing impact on the church and its missionary enterprise.

-> "Voice-print" technology will make keyboards obsolete. We will carry computers in our pockets, talk to them, and they will talk to us.

-> World prayer conferences, evangelism events, and missions conferences will simultaneously unite tens of millions, or even billions of people worldwide through satellite and fiber optic networks.

-> Teleconferencing of missionaries with their leaders and missionary leaders with each other will save millions in travel costs and promote networking at an unprecedented level.

-> Missiological and theological libraries consisting of tens of thousands of books will be available on CD-ROM disks with many gigabytes of storage capacity.

-> The new technology will allow decentralized, yet rapid collection and dissemination of information on the church, cultures, target peoples, and missionary personnel from all points of the globe. Missionary leaders will be able to make decisions based upon real-time data collection and analysis. Data from hundreds of sources around the globe may be collected, input, processed, analyzed, and used in the field all in the same day.

As the ability to transmit information across political boundaries increases, it will bring power and economic opportunities to peoples in countries previously cut off from competition in the global marketplace. This will lead to a major reconstitution of political entities, and new opportunities for the Gospel will continue to emerge.

Generally, political and economic factors have not had a strong determining influence on the growth of the church in the non-Western world. It has been able to flourish in both liberal and totalitarian societies. But such factors have had a determining influence on the growth and impact of missions movements in the non-Western world. Political controls on foreign travel, for instance, have had a major impact on the non-Western church's ability to send foreign missionaries. As such controls over the cross-fertilization of both ideas and peoples diminish, the growth of the missions movement in the non-Western world promises to be spectacular.

Already, recent research demonstrates that the non-Western missions movement is 35.5 percent of the Protestant total and is growing five times faster than the missions movement in the Western world.[3]

Figure 16.1 compares the growth of these two movements. It also demonstrates that, if present trends continue, there will be more missionaries from non-Western peoples (55 percent of the total) than from Western churches by the year 2000.

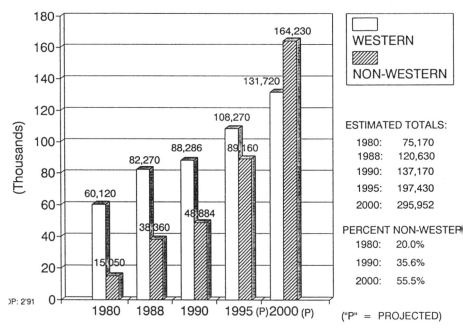

GLOBAL PROTESTANT MISSIONARIES

WESTERN
NON-WESTERN

ESTIMATED TOTALS:

1980:	75,170
1988:	120,630
1990:	137,170
1995:	197,430
2000:	295,952

PERCENT NON-WESTER

1980:	20.0%
1990:	35.6%
2000:	55.5%

("P" = PROJECTED)

Figure 16.1

This is a new reality. Churches and mission agencies around the world must work to create new ways of relating to each other, accomplishing the work and demonstrating the nature of the Kingdom together, and providing moral and ethical answers to the masses and power elite of the world.

Partnership is the generic term which best describes the basket of new relationships which must emerge in a global church with a global mission. We will hear and use this term much more in the future. It will encompass topics as diverse as spiritual unity and organizational diversity, mission associations and unreached peoples, nonresident missionaries and task-focused cooperation. We need to learn to embrace this word and its meaning more fully.

Reflections on the Consultation

This Working Consultation on Partnership for World Evangelism marks the beginning of what may become a series of international meetings on missionary partnership. The subject of cooperation, or partnership, increasingly is emerging as a necessary kernel of strategy for the future. The closer we focus on the specific tasks of world evangelism, the more we see the necessity of partnership. Churches and mission agencies have too many vital tasks they cannot do without cooperation with each other. Countries can best be surveyed, missionaries can best be trained, and unreached peoples can best be evangelized through cooperative efforts.

Focusing upon Task Demands Partnership

In October, 1992, two or three leaders of each country in Latin America were to convene a consultation to focus on a specific task. The intent was to lead the evangelical churches of twenty-three Ibero-American countries to "adopt," or assume the responsibility for the evangelization of at least 3,000 unreached people groups. This effort can only be successful as Latin Americans develop a strong sense of cooperative responsibility and a practical determination to unify their efforts to achieve such goals.

The rising interest in cooperative partnership efforts is a healthy indication that the evangelical church is becoming serious about accomplishing the remaining tasks of world evangelization. A desire for partnership places tasks above organizations. That can be very healthy in this age of transition for the missionary enterprise.

Emerging Concepts for Partnership

The Wheaton Consultation schedule allowed both the speakers and the consultation delegates to make significant contributions to the proceedings. The consultation was evenly balanced between time given for presentations on concepts and on models. But it was also balanced by giving equal time both to the working group sessions and to the presentations and models. One-half of the consultation time was given to working group sessions. This made for healthy interaction and significant contributions by both presenters and delegates alike. The following discussion highlights some of the most important topics and results of the consultation.

The Biblical Basis of Partnership

Many of the contributors at the consultation chose pertinent biblical passages to introduce the concept of partnership. A summary of some of the most important is instructive:

1. Eccles. 4:9,12. Synergy — two can accomplish more than twice as much as one, and three is even better! (Panya Baba)

2. I Cor. 3:9. Community — believers are both a means and an object of partnership ministry. (Panya Baba)

3. Rom. 12; I Cor. 12; Eph. 4. Integrated Assets Model — the integration of "body" parts so that the whole may function is a powerful scriptural analogy demanding partnership. (Phill Butler)

4. Phil. 1. Comprehensive — Biblical models involving prayer, mobilization, and finances. (Luis Bush)

These few examples demonstrate that many theological treasures yet remain to be mined under the banner of partnership. Our understanding of the biblical data has been impaired by our inability to see much beyond Western models of partnership. Fortunately, the growing globalization of world evangelism and emerging new models promise to enrich our theological understanding of partnership.

Characteristics of Effective Partnerships

It is instructive to discover what the working groups of the consultation had in common in their descriptions of effective partnerships. For half the consultation, these groups convened independently and represented a wide variety of church and missions leaders. Yet a close examination of their work reveals many common descriptions of effective partnerships. The following appeared in the results of two or more of these working groups:

> *prayerful leadership*
> *spiritual leadership/maturity*
> *mutual respect and trust*
> *theological compatibility*
> *commitment to common goals*
> *adequate communication*
> *honesty*
> *common goals/goal ownership*
> *acceptance of cultural differences*
> *flexibility*
> *goal/task-oriented*
> *clear and realistic expectations*
> *willingness to forgive*
> *servant leadership*
> *dependability*
> *interdependence, not paternalism*
> *willingness to sacrifice*
> *shared success or failure*

This partial list is sufficient to sense the healthy depth of discussion in this consultation. These descriptives above would make good discussion topics in many church and missions meetings, but they are vital for the development of healthy partnerships internationally.

Notice how many of the descriptives allude to the importance of building interpersonal relationships between partners. This is a theme which constantly recurs in the minds of those experienced in developing international partnerships. For instance, partnership emerged as the theme of the triannual meeting of the World Evangelical Fellowship Missions Commission held in the Philippines in June, 1992. According to William Taylor, Executive Secretary of the Missions Commission, selected Western and non-Western leaders from around the world represented mission agencies, movements, and associations of agencies in this "working consultation."

The "overarching" goals of the WEF meetings were:

- To build bridges and trust
- To build bridges of relationships
- To build networks
- To build specific partnership relationships

Note that three of the four purposes listed have to do with building trust relationships between leaders. This strongly felt need among those working in partnership and in developing partnerships cannot be ignored by church and mission leaders who would enter the arena of partnership development.

Theoretical Contributions of the Wheaton Consultation

In my opinion, two major theoretical contributions to our understanding of partnership emerged from this consultation. The first appeared in some of the papers and models presented. The second emerged out of discussion in one of the working groups. The first is called the "enosis" concept by Moats and "horizontal-vertical integration" by Butler. Both are essentially the same principle, and they have been given articulation by both Isaachar and Interdev. Butler explains the concept most clearly, and Moats lists some excellent concomitant principles.

Christian missions, says Butler, have traditionally concentrated on horizontal integration. Certain "ministries" and their corresponding organizations have developed ministry specialties and carried them on in many parts of the world; e.g., Bible societies, radio ministries, literature ministries, crusade evangelism ministries, and the like. Increasing the value of such ministries has essentially been defined in terms of horizontal expansion to larger geographical spheres.

Butler and Moats demonstrate the importance of "vertical integration" in a day when the majority of the unreached peoples of the world are in the Hindu, Muslim, and Buddhist populations. We should concentrate the resources of many "ministries" by vertically integrating them for the purpose of reaching one people group or region at a time.

This is not just theory. The Elmbrook Church's experience in vertically integrated partnership and the partnerships developed by Issachar are testimony to the importance of this concept. In his presentation Phill Butler summarized Interdev's current activity in developing such partnerships.

More recently, partnerships focused on specific language groups date back to about 1985. Today, to our knowledge, there are seven of these partnerships operating with more than 200 partner agencies involved. The good news is that about 35 percent of these partner ministries are non-Western. Some of the partnerships are made up of 100 percent national or Two-Thirds world agencies. In addition to these seven operational partnerships, probably another five or six are in various stages of formation. And perhaps another ten or twelve are being discussed.

The concept of vertically integrated partnerships is a major theoretical advance in our understanding of partnership. It focuses upon bringing together personnel and resources from many dissimilar ministries to focus upon one central task. As Butler points out, this type of model is not entirely new. But when combined with the vertical integration concept, it provides both a conceptual and practical framework for multiplying a higher order of partnership efforts. Other organizations would do well to consider how this concept might be applied to their own plans for partnership.

The second significant theoretical insight emerged in the working session meeting of Two-Thirds world missions partnerships. I am referring to the relationship between economic resources and response to the gospel, and how they impact partnership needs and development. The graphic matrix on page 155 serves to explain some history, needs, and priorities of partnership development. For example:

1. **Partnership as a distant option (A):** The high (gospel) response-high resources areas of the world are found in the upper right quadrant of the matrix. They have tended toward horizontal integration and unilateral gospel outreach. In these regions of the world, the church tends toward decentralized, independent Christian institutions and efforts. Partnership tends to be viewed as a relatively unimportant option. The Church here has the resources to support this sectarian, horizontal mode of witness. Partnerships which have developed in this part of the world are few in relationship to resources, and they tend to protect organizational autonomy.

2. **Partnership as necessity (B):** Low response-low resource regions of the world are in the lower left quadrant of the matrix. The church in these regions cannot make significant progress in its witness without significant help from the outside. The need for partnership is

obvious to its leaders, but they do not have the resources and access to other parts of the world even to develop partnership possibilities. Partnerships in these regions of the world tend to be based more upon necessity, and they are community and survival oriented. The leaders of churches in this region would welcome opportunities for well conceived and administered partnerships with the churches outside.

3. **Partnership as social responsibility (C):** Low response-high resources regions belong in the upper left quadrant of the matrix. The church in these regions of the world tends toward declining numbers and influence with the societies of these regions. It is far more open to partnership development than the church in high response-high resource regions, but the partnerships developed tend toward community development activities more than overt evangelistic activities.

4. **Partnership as paternalism (D):** High response-low resources regions are represented by the lower right quadrant of the matrix. The church in these regions recognizes a strong need for partnerships, but historically, they have suffered under the paternalism of colonialism. They tend to welcome partnerships, but they zealously guard against entering into real or perceived paternalistic relationships which they know can be disguised by the word partnership. They are open but wary. Partnerships in these regions, though difficult to develop, can have rapid and fruitful results.

This matrix helps us understand the difficulties and opportunities related to partnership development in various countries and regions of the world and how they are affected by the economic and spiritual context. It explains why it has historically been more difficult to develop partnerships between certain regions. It also demonstrates the need for more partnerships between the top and bottom halves of the matrix.

Resources Needed for Partnership Development

When most people think of the transfer of partnership resources, they automatically think of money. But what is not usually considered adequately is the personnel resources necessary to develop and maintain partnerships.

Phill Butler, speaking from the experience of Interdev, makes a strong case for the development of specialists who work in partnership development full-time. If there is any theme which recurred consistently in the working groups, it is the fact that partnerships develop as a result of relationship and trust. Establishing those relationships necessary for partnerships to form and continue requires considerable skill and experience. To see such skills develop in the global community, Interdev is now sponsoring two-week intensive training seminars for those interested in this specialized ministry. The Peoples Mission International has also recognized the strategic importance of partnership development. A special department is being established solely for the purpose of developing strategic partnerships around the world. Those interested in this area of ministry would do well to review the qualifications listed in the results of the Church-to-Church and Mission-to-Mission Partnership working groups in Chapters 9 and 12.

Financially, a number of nontraditional sources for partnership are emerging. One of the primary trends is church-to-church and church-to-mission partnerships. Like Elmbrook, scores of churches, primarily in North America, Asia, and Latin America, are successfully experimenting with church-based partnering. As Elmbrook has confirmed, however, the motivation for church-based partnering should not be to bypass mission agencies. Most missionary activities have much more in common with each other than not, and the church cannot afford to replace nor ignore the expertise to be found in mission agencies.

Two-Thirds World Missions Partnership Priorities

It is interesting to note the list of action-step priorities under development by the Two-Thirds world missions working group. Partnership in providing education for Two-Thirds world missionary children would not appear on a Western missionary leader's list of priorities. Neither would a call for an international network of Christian entrepreneurs interested in generating resources for Two-Thirds world missions.

It appears to be almost universally recognized that a need for international cooperation in training Two-Thirds world missionaries is of critical importance. Organizations such as the World Evangelical Fellowship Missions Commission, OC International (USA), Mision Mundiales (Argentina), COMIBAM (Latin America), the Asian Missions Commission, the Missions Commission of the Association of Evangelical Churches of Africa and Madagascar, and a number of other prominent organizations are now implementing ministries to address this need. The size and growth of the Two-Thirds world missions movement demands that denominational and independent mission agencies around the world give this need a priority in their strategic planning.

The Excluded Middle of Missionary Partnerships

A tremendous need exists for ministries which partner with the Two-Thirds world missions movement to rapidly reproduce effective strategies for evangelizing unreached peoples. Those who minister to the Two-Thirds world missions movement on an international scale can best be described as falling somewhere along a continuum.

On one end of the continuum are those agencies which function primarily to channel funds to the Two-Thirds world missions movement. To varying degrees, these funding organizations require of their recipients accountability for *funding*, but give little accountability for the *task*. Generally, the receiving agencies make their own plans for ministry and simply receive assistance to carry out those plans by these funding organizations. The major funding agencies of this type are Christian Aid Mission (A), Gospel for Asia (B), and Partners International (C).

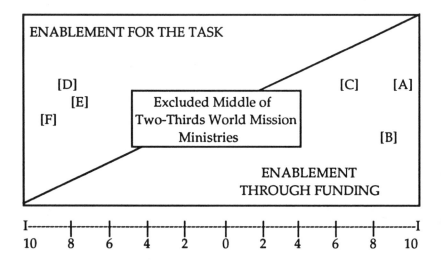

The Excluded Middle of Ministries to Two-Thirds World Missions

Figure 16.2

On the other end of the continuum lie ministries which give little or no funding to the Two-Thirds world missions movement, but are active in various ministries which provide assistance and expertise related to the task of cross-cultural ministry. These ministries present Two-Thirds world missions with maximum accountability for the *task*. Those on the other end of the continuum provide accountability for the funds.

The **Two-Thirds World Missions Ministries (TWM)** of OC International (D) has been ministering to the Two-Thirds world missions movement in this manner since 1984. The similar strategies of Interdev [E] and Issachar [F] also represent help with the task, but little or no funding.

The middle of the continuum has largely been excluded from the efforts of major international mission agencies. There is no international organization existing to provide major assistance in designing strategies while at the same time providing assistance in funding the resulting missionary projects.

Those organizations on the right of the continuum feel safe from exercising paternalistic control over the indigenous agencies with which they partner because they work hard to avoid the appearance of controlling their strategies. Those on the left end of the continuum feel equally comfortable in avoiding paternalistic dominance because they offer consulting services without ongoing financial assistance.

Organizations on both sides of the continuum are probably deluding themselves in their attempts to avoid paternalism. As is evident in the list of characteristics concerning effective partnerships above, paternalism has more to do with attitudes and interpersonal relationships than it does the type of assistance offered by partnering agencies.

Furthermore, since the partnership needs of the non-Western world are vast in almost every sphere, organizations on both sides of the continuum are engaged in effective ministries. Seldom is the charge of paternalism leveled at these agencies from the non-Western world. They are too much in demand. Since both sides of the continuum are represented by effective ministries and enjoy a generally positive reputation in the Two-Thirds world, there is no reason why international organizations could not purposely offer ministry on both ends of the continuum. What better agency to help build financial partnership than the one which also partnered in the development of effective strategies? It is this focus which has brought the Peoples Mission International into existence.

Effective ministry to the Two-Thirds world missions movement requires *both* assistance in focusing on the task and in establishing funding partnerships. The most effective help to the movement would include ministries which help Two-Thirds world leaders focus on the critical targets of effective missionary ministry, develop contextualized, practical strategies, and produce resources from around the world (including their own context) to accomplish those tasks. Such focused ministry would help these leaders design their strategies and monitor their progress.

In the coming age of global missions, the actual multiplication of believers and churches among unreached peoples will be more important than where all the resources come from. Ministries must serve to help Two-Thirds world missions leaders develop the best possible and most comprehensive strategies to evangelize specific people groups. They must also serve to partner the required personnel and resources to successfully implement the task. This would provide maximum assistance and accountability for both the task and the resources.

Conclusion

As the church prepares for the twenty-first century, it will increasingly think of itself in global terms. The communications revolution and the resulting rapid economic, political, and social globalization will bring unprecedented challenges and opportunities for a church which is prepared. As the political and economic status quo is challenged by technological revolution, the church will be equally challenged by its own growth and globalization trends.

In the minds of many missionary and church leaders, partnership spells the way forward for the coming age. The Church has always struggled with defining its mission and its nature; what the church is to *BE* in the world, as well as what it is to *DO* in the world. Christ linked the two together inseparably in His priestly prayer to the Father, "May they be brought to complete unity that the world may know that you have sent me." (John 17:23)

Those who have emphasized *being* over *doing* have become confused in the attempt to achieve organizational unity at the expense of the Church's mission. The resulting organizational unity was an empty shell without a message for the world.

Those who have emphasized *doing* over *being* have attempted to accomplish independently what can effectively only be accomplished in unity. The result has too often been triumphalistic organizational lip-service which falls far short of establishing the Church Jesus came to build.

Partnership can form an effective bridge between being and doing. Effectively developed partnerships can synthesize the unified efforts of mission and church organizations. It is not unity *for* mission, but unity *in* mission which is the essence of Christ's prayer. That spells the need for partnership development on a scale and in ways we may not have even considered to this point. Just as there is a shake-out of political and economic organizations underway in the information age, so there will be a shake-out of church and mission structures in the coming age of globalization. In both arenas, those which survive and flourish will likely be those which turn partnering into both an art and a science.

Endnotes

[1] David McKenna, *Mega Truth, The Church In The Age of Information*, San Bernardino, Here's Life Publishers, 1986, 14.

[2] "Into 21st Century", *Futurist*, July-August 1988.

[3] Larry D. Pate, "The Changing Balance In Global Mission," *International Bulletin of Missionary Research*, Vol 15, No 2, April 1991, 60.

Section 7

❖❖❖

Appendices

APPENDIX A

Consultation Resolution

Partnership for World Evangelization
A Working Consultation
The Billy Graham Center, Wheaton College
May 11, 1991

Acknowledging that God in these days as never before has brought together concerned individuals, churches, mission agencies, and organizations to seek fruitful partnerships for world evangelization, and

Realizing the critical need for much more effective worldwide evangelization, and

Confessing our need for personal holiness and courage, our need to practice the unity Jesus called for in John 17, and our need for God's wisdom and direction, without which all our partnership efforts will be futile,

We, the participants in the Working Consultation on Partnership For World Evangelization, meeting at the Billy Graham Center, Wheaton College, May 9-11, 1991, hereby **affirm**

... our continued obedience to Christ's Great Commission in the midst of a rapidly changing world, which gives us many new strategic opportunities to take the gospel to the ends of the earth;

... the interdependence of all parts of the Body of Jesus Christ, the Church, and the reciprocal nature of all partnerships;

... the witness to our unity in Christ provided by mission partnerships;

... our desire to live by the biblical principles and patterns for partnership in world mission;

... that the effectiveness and integrity of our mission are demonstrated by our partnerships;

... the viability and applicability of many models of partnership that have been singularly blessed by God for the effective furtherance of the gospel, bringing together (a) ministry coalitions on the field; (b) churches on all continents; (c) Western agencies and Two-Thirds world agencies, and (d) Two-Thirds world agencies with other Two-Thirds world agencies;

... the necessity to change long-standing indifference toward partnerships, so they will be seen not as luxuries but as utter necessities;

... that consistent, fervent prayer is needed, to join our Lord in his prayer for oneness which is found in him alone;

... that the work of the Holy Spirit is essential to bring about the mutual trust that is the foundation of all successful partnerships;

... that patience and perseverance are needed to effect partnerships;

... the necessity to guard against all forms of dominance, both overt and subtle, in all partnerships;

and we hereby commit ourselves to explore and develop new partnerships for world evangelization, so that

... all remaining unreached and least evangelized peoples will be reached;

... missions-active churches will be planted among those peoples;

... all churches, agencies, movements, institutions, and structures will be better mobilized toward the fulfillment of the Great Commission.

APPENDIX B

Current State of Partnership in Missions in Asia

2-1. Interview with Rev. Koji Ishikawa, General Secretary of Japan Evangelical Association (JEA), April 3, 1991, in Seoul

1. Please describe the recent missions movement in Japan with the number of missionaries and missions societies.

About 400 Japanese cross-cultural missionaries are presently working around the world. There were 270 missionaries two years ago. The 400 Japanese missionaries have been sent out through about 10 missions agencies and 15 denominational missions committees. Evangelical Alliance Church, for example, sent out 21 missionaries. More missionaries have been sent out through denominations than through societies.

2. How effective is the cooperative effort for missions among denominations and agencies?

There is a kind of cooperation, but it is not yet enough. Japan Overseas Missions Association (JOMA) includes most of the denominations and agencies. The cooperation is not yet deep, but at the level of exchanging information and holding missions sessions together twice a year.

If a certain Japanese joins Overseas Missionary Fellowship (OMF) and goes out to the field, he belongs to OMF and obeys OMF policies. The OMF has a very strong policy. Denominations do not have administrative responsibilities but only support OMF missionaries through prayer and finances. There is no real cooperation.

Wycliffe Bible Translators also has its own policy but not as strong as OMF. When a Japanese joins Wycliffe, he is supervised both by Wycliffe and his denomination. His denomination not only supports through prayer and finances but also participates in a certain policy-making process.

The Evangelical Alliance as a denomination bears all of the responsibilities for the missionaries such as prayer, finances, and policy making. But the Evangelical Alliance Church establishes field councils on each mission field, and the field council controls missionaries in the field. The Alliance Church at home and the Alliance Council in the field maintain good cooperation.

If a Japanese goes out as a missionary through Evangelical Alliance Church to Indonesia, he or she is supported through prayer and finances by the Evangelical Alliance Church at home and is controlled by the Alliance Field Council in Indonesia in the matter of administrative policy making. The Alliance Field Council also cooperates with Indonesian Churches. Indonesian Church leaders participate in the Field Council and the Japanese missionaries cooperate with Indonesian Churches in their ministries.

3. Would Evangelical Fellowship of Asia (EFA) or Asian Mission Association (AMA) help your national missions movement?

The EFA could provide some information and encouragement. But JEA can provide most of the encouragement and help for Japanese Churches to cooperate.

4. How does your national missions association cooperate with your churches and missions societies?

No. Japan Overseas Missions Association (JOMA) only provides fellowship, exchange of information, and studies. Each denomination and each agency has its own policy and carries out its own policy independently. They have their own money, and they use it. JOMA does not yet provide a forum in which missions policies are evaluated and adjusted. Of course Japanese Churches are facing many issues in missions. They do not yet know how to overcome these issues together.

5. Is there any conflict between Japanese churches and Western mission societies?

Yes, there is. First of all, the Westerners and Japanese have different cultures. So they have their own policies.

Secondly, even though the Japanese and the Westerners in the Alliance Church are officially one and publicly working together in Japan, inside there are two groups. The missionaries have their own annual conferences, and Japanese churches also have their own annual conferences. Of course we study together and exchange information, but we are not really working together.

Thirdly, such missions agencies as OMF control financial and legal matters as well as policy making. This is mainly because they are more experienced, and the Japanese churches do not have as much knowledge. The Western missionaries usually take initiatives in missions. But Japanese churches are beginning to study how to do this.

It is the right time for the Japanese churches to study and learn. We hope we can grow and cooperate together.

6. *Is there any need of cooperation among Third-World churches?*
Yes. Japanese Churches need cooperation through JOMA under JEA.

7. *Any suggestions for cooperation?*
1) We should know each other more. We should know the situations better.
2) We should share together. What kind of programs do we have? How can we overcome such issues? We need more specific information.
3) We should try to learn how to work together. Cooperation means fifty-fifty, same-level partnership. We have just begun to discuss and exchange information.

2-2. Dr. Kunimitsu Ogawa (Evangelical Free Church in Japan)

1. *Can you describe the recent growth of the foreign missionary movement in Japan with number of missionaries and missions agencies?*
The number of missionaries has been growing although the missions agencies are not increasing in number. It is interesting to observe that more women than men have been preparing themselves for foreign missions.

2. *How effective is your cooperative effort among churches and missions agencies in your country? Do you have the national missions association to represent many missions agencies?*
JOMA holds the annual retreat for new missionary candidates. I was the main speaker at the most recent retreat sponsored by JOMA.

3. *What can AMA and EFA Missions Commission do to help your national missionary movement and missions association?*
One of the most important roles of missions associations would be to help the sending churches and the receiving churches have a deeper fellowship and understanding in order to develop cooperation and partnership in missions.

4. How can your national missions associations cooperate with denominations and missions associations from the West?

Cooperation has steadily developed between national missions associations and denominations. But there is still a gap that needs to be met. One of the keys is to have the right mediators from both parties. Western missions agencies have been operating quite independently from the national missions association except for some organization.

5. Do you see a need to promote cooperation among missions agencies in the Third World?

Yes, I do. But the goal should be to promote fellowship and cooperation among Asian Churches.

6. What about the issues and problems?

Parachurch missions associations have been rather aggressive and threatening to the local churches and denominations. A servant attitude needs to be established from both sides.

2-3. Interview with Dr. Chun Chae Ok (professor at Ewha Women's University), April 3, 1991, Seoul, Korea

1. Please describe the recent missions movement in Korea with the number of missionaries and missions societies.

I would like to talk mainly about OMF. OMF has a 12-year history in Korea and presently sends out 20 missionary families. The Korean OMF council provides the personnel, finances, and prayer support but does not actively participate in the policy making of the OMF headquarters.

2. Is there a cooperation and partnership established between the Korean missionaries and the OMF?

The Korean missionaries in the field do not really have cooperation and partnership with the Western missionaries. They are even discriminated against. It is not because the OMF has a policy of defying and pressing the Korean missionaries but mainly because the Korean missionaries are lacking in abilities; that is, language training and missionary experience. The Korean missionaries are just beginners and do not yet know how to cope with international missionary mentality.

The Korean OMF Council has reached international standing, yet its opinions are not yet actively reflected at the headquarters. After all, the OMF, which has been structured as West-centered, decides all the policies. In a word, real partnership is not yet established or practiced. The Korean missionaries are sent out through the Korean OMF Council, but they are actually controlled both by the OMF headquarters and the OMF field council. Of course it is desirable and practical for the Korean missionaries to be controlled by the fully experienced OMF; yet sometimes it is necessary that some creative opinions and proposals be reflected on. Some Korean missionaries even hesitate to express their viewpoints for they are afraid that they might be regarded as disobedient and lacking in faith.

3. Is there cooperation between the Korean denominations and the missions societies in Korea?

No. There is lots of waste in terms of personnel and money. Almost every denomination and every missions agency carries out its own program and projects for missions independently. An Association of Missions Societies has been formed in Korea. It is, however, regretful that it has done almost nothing for real cooperation in missions. This formation of a missions association was made in a competitive, superficial, and rushed manner by well known, over-loaded, church leaders so that it has been unable to coordinate local churches and missionaries in the field. There has been competition rather than real cooperation and partnership among missions societies. This has burned up resources and energies for missions.

It is high time for the Korean Church to demonstrate the unity of the church. And mission is the best way through which the oneness of the church is practiced. There have been all kinds of sporadic missions movements and organizations. But they have not been coordinated.

In a sense it is a time of crisis in missions. A moderate, even small-scale, practical cooperation among missions leaders should be attempted. This is not a time when we should go out to promote missions movements. It is rather a time when we should establish a system and the right atmosphere to coordinate and support field missionaries and home churches.

Such a system or missions association should include a number of field missionaries who have a genuine love for the field and an understanding of it. The newly formed Korea World Missions Association should provide a forum at which various missions organizations can be coordinated and where united missions seminars and training programs can be developed. As a result, duplication of training programs could be eliminated. The KWMA should also provide a channel through which a great number of female personnel could be encouraged to participate in missions.

4. Why is cooperation and partnership in missions needed?
First of all, this is the age of internationalization. Secondly, the ministry is becoming more diversified and mutually related. One cannot therefore insist on one's own unique ministry. Thirdly, in this age of religious and ideological plurality, a demonstration of Christian and ministerial unity is crucial for evangelism. Fourthly, in the light of the coming age of unification in Korea, the practice of cooperation and partnership is imperative.

For these reasons, we Koreans have to cultivate our abilities. It is not because we are not intelligent. It is mainly because we have not been properly trained. At the same time we have to possess love. Abilities and love should go together, and they are basic for missions and for partnership. We also have to humbly learn from the history of Western missions, including the history of the Catholic missionaries. When we go out to the field, we should not neglect all the previous work done by the Western missionaries. We should not behave as if we are the first pioneers on an uninhabited island.

5. What do you want to say to the Western missions leaders?
Western missions leaders individually do their best to overcome Western ways, but as a group they are still bound to the Western mentality. The West should take a more humble attitude. Partnership cannot be established unless both parties come to equal and practical terms. The West should not just be proud of its past history but should come down to equal terms to establish a real cooperation and partnership. While we have to learn and cultivate our ability, they also have to learn and cultivate humility.

2-4. Interview with Dr. Marlin Nelson (a missionary and professor at ACTS, Seoul), April 3, 1991, Seoul, Korea

1. Please describe some different patterns of missions in relation to cooperation and partnership. Which is the best pattern?
There are three kinds of patterns in which Korean missionaries are already engaged. The first pattern is a diaspora missions; that is,

Korean missionaries working with Koreans in other countries. They are doing very well and are most successful.

The second pattern is when the Korean missionaries join international missions societies such as OMF, SIM, and OM and go out to the field.

The third pattern is when the Korean missionaries go out independently to the field to form Korean mission societies, plant churches, and start new denominations. In this case they ignore the existing churches, and as we often say, "reinvent the wheel," and start doing everything all over again.

The fourth pattern which I do recommend is that the Korean missionaries go out to the field and relate themselves with the existing evangelical indigenous churches. By becoming a partner with an evangelical national church, the missionaries could inspire national churches. In that way missions would not be regarded as merely foreign but rather a cooperative international gospel team.

What I say is that Korean missionaries should join indigenous churches and establish partnership with them. If the missionaries do not cooperate with the national church but instead establish their own church, and if God blesses their ministry, then the field people will expect the missionaries to become their pastors. I do not believe the missionaries should become pastors in the field. Missionaries should encourage national churches to grow but should not take on their responsibilities. By practicing cooperation and partnership, missionaries can demonstrate that Christianity is not a foreign religion but an international religion and also demonstrate the oneness of the Body. This is a tremendous witness.

2. What is the role of the missionaries in the field? Do they have to relate to the international missions society to which they belong before they relate to the national church?

In the case of SIM and many other missions societies, they have already created their own denominations and churches. The SIM is already a church in the field. Therefore if a missionary goes out to the field and relates himself to SIM, that will be enough. In the case of some other international missions societies, they do not establish denominations but work independently or in cooperation with national churches.

3. Who should send out missionaries or through which body should one go out to the field?

The first case is that missionaries are sent out by denominations. The missions committee should study the field to find out the need. This committee should find the right persons and send them to the field. Local churches should provide financial and prayer support through the denomination, according to the established salary, rather than sending at random.

In the second case missionaries are sent out through international missions societies such as SIM and OMF. There are advantages as well as disadvantages in this case.

The third case is that local churches send out missionaries and expect them to start churches or seminaries all by themselves. In this case a few dozen other local churches which receive prayer letters from the missionary also could send financial support directly to the missionaries without knowing that other churches are sending money. All of the money may be well used, but it can also become a temptation. The missionary in this case could put some money in his private bank account while he puts other money in his missions account. The third case is the poorest one.

If a Korean missionary feels called to work with an international missions society, he will apply to them through a local branch of that missions society. He will be evaluated, trained, and selected. He will raise money according to the policy of that mission society. If he joins that organization he should be controlled by it. He must follow their policy, not that of his denomination.

If a Korean missionary feels called to work with his denomination, he should apply to the denomination. In this case the missions board of his denomination should develop a good policy with adequate finances, schooling, medical care, retirement, and all these things. To me this is the biggest problem. It is because denominations do not have experience while international missions societies do have hundreds of years of experience.

The only problem with the societies is that the Asian is in the minority in the Western international organization. So the main task with the denomination is to learn how to improve their missionary selection, training, sending, supervision, and finances of those sent by their denomination.

4. I don't think you stress the need to establish a kind of policy making agreement between denominational missions committees and international missions societies.

No. What I would like to emphasize most is to develop cooperation and partnership between sending church and field church regardless of whether the missionaries are sent out by a denomination or a missions society.

2-5. Rev. Daniel Ho, General Secretary of National Evangelical Christian Fellowship (NECF) in Malaysia

1. Please describe the recent missions movement in Malaysia with the number of missionaries and missions societies.

There has been slow but steady growth. Most of our missionaries go out with OMF, SIM, Interserve, Operation Mobilization (short-term), Youth With A Mission (short-term), and Wycliffe Bible Translators. Most foreign missions agencies work here, while denominational missions committees are few.

2. How effective is your cooperative effort among churches and mission agencies in your country? Do you have a national missions association to represent many missions agencies?

There is increasing cooperation, and NECF in Malaysia is spearheading this. We are in the process of forming a national missions association.

3. What can EFA Missions Commission or AMA do to help your national missionary movement and missions association?

Provide good resource materials and personnel to teach, train, and challenge locals regarding missions needs and strategies.

4. How can your national missions association cooperate with denominations and missions associations from the West?

There should be greater consultation and cooperation. There should be respect and sensitivity to each other's needs and peculiarities.

5. Do you see a need to promote cooperation among missions agencies in the third world?

Yes!

6. What about the issues and problems?

There would still be the cross-cultural issues and problems. But if missions can be divested from being associated with the West only, it would help a fair amount in missions and making the Gospel of Christ known.

2-6. Dr. Octavianus, President of Indonesian Missionary Fellowship

1. Can you describe the recent growth of the foreign missionary movement in Indonesia with number of missionaries and missions agencies?

Information on the foreign missionary movement in Indonesia is not solid. Foreign missionaries to Indonesia come with a variety of sponsorship and legal guises, although all are sponsored by a national organization. Foreign missions now working in Indonesia include TEAM, Inter-Varsity, Campus Crusade for Christ, Navigators, Bethany Fellowship, Christian Literature Crusade, WEC, Southern Baptist, RBMU, Go Ye Fellowship, OMF, OMS, Norwegian Lutheran Mission, World Vision, Gospel Recordings, New Tribes Mission, and Summer Institute of Linguistics (Wycliffe).

Asian missions operations in Indonesia include Korea Internationale Mission, Korea Evangelical Mission, and Japan Antioch Mission. The development of foreign missions in Indonesia is limited by the Indonesian government. Strict quotas exist on the number of foreigners whose visas may be sponsored by Indonesian organizations, and all missionaries end up working closely with an Indonesian organization, church, or school.

Indonesian missions agencies are very few. Indonesian Missionary Fellowship is the largest organization sending missionaries abroad, with a current target of sending 20 new missionaries abroad in the next four years. Other efforts known to us are entirely limited to sending Indonesian pastors to Indonesian ethic groups outside the country, rather than doing cross-cultural evangelism and church planting.

2. How effective is your cooperative effort among churches and missions agencies in your country? Do you have a national missions association to represent many missions agencies?

Cooperation between churches and missions in Indonesia varies greatly. Within the conciliar churches, cooperation occurs by the transfer of funds, almost exclusively, but quite limited. The cooperation in evangelical churches may be strong or weak, depending on the situation.

Denominations which cooperate with churches in Indonesia include the Southern Baptists, the Norwegian Lutherans, and the

C&MA. The relationships in all these organizations can become strained over issues of culture and theology, but are generally harmonious. Most evangelical missions tend to work only within the denominations they have founded, and cooperation seems to be best where there is a clear definition of the missionary's role. Indonesia's national missions organization is the Fellowship of Indonesian Missions, a branch of the Evangelical Fellowship of Indonesia. That organization helps to encourage cooperation and partnership, but does not have a very high profile in the country.

3. What can AMA and EFA Missions Commission do to help your national missionary movement and missions association?

So far AMA and EFA have had a limited involvement in Indonesia, with roles which are largely coordinative and consultative. At present there is not much felt need for a more active role from these two organizations, although any initiative on their part would be quite welcome.

4. How can your national missions association cooperate with denominations and missions associations from the West?

Cooperation among mission-minded organizations in Indonesia is theoretical. Indonesian churches and missions tend to be divided along denominational lines, though there is little outright conflict. Although we share a universal task, we do not see a large amount of cooperative initiative. Indonesian Missionary Fellowship is somewhat an exception to that pattern, because it not only receives foreign missionaries, but also sends Indonesians as missionaries abroad. IMF seeks to work across denominational lines (with varying levels of success) and to be a bridge for understanding and cooperation. But existing as a nondenominational entity is difficult in Indonesia.

5. Do you see a need to promote cooperation among missions agencies in the Third World?

Asians need to cooperate in missions, but the form of cooperation needs to be guarded carefully with respect to the political context. In Indonesia, a large public gathering of organizations dedicated to evangelism would be politically foolish. Far better would be the formation of some voluntary association which could arrange small gatherings and quiet operation. Missions agencies of the Third World do need to learn to cooperate and to face the challenges of independence and responsibility. The Asia Missions Congress (AMC) of 1990 was a great step in that direction for Asia.

6. What about the issues and problems?

Issues and problems in Indonesia include:

1) Re-Islamization. The majority religion in Indonesia has settled on the goal of establishing, not an Islamic state, but a religious community which rules the country by influence. By subtle and diligent means, they have introduced a marriage law based upon their religious principles, they have established government-recognized religious courts, reintroduced certain attire in the schools, and influenced the country's higher education system. Their efforts at present include making Arabic one of the national languages, strengthening their "Intellectual Association," and influencing particularly the government on Java.

2) Lack of evangelical favor in the churches. Most Indonesian Churches are not open to the evangelistic power of the Holy Spirit. They are content with biological growth in membership only and so have become stagnant. The denominations and churches which are open and seeking to grow are indeed growing at a fast pace, but they represent a minority of churches. In addition, among churches, seminaries, and parachurch organizations, there can be an unhealthy spirit of rivalry which hurts the testimony of Christ and the growth of His kingdom.

3) Indonesia's training institutions are in serious need of qualified indigenous educators. In evangelical institutions, there are perhaps five Indonesian teachers with earned doctorates. The liberal institutions are full of teachers with doctorates, because the mainline denominations are ready to help with scholarships and other forms of aid, but evangelicals have not proven so generous towards the needs of evangelical higher education.

2-7. Rev. Edmond Mok, Hong Kong Association of Christian Missions

1. Can you describe the recent growth of the foreign missionary movement in Hong Kong with number of missionaries and missions agencies?

There was a rapid growth in the 1980s. But recently the growth has slowed down. Right now there are 97 missionaries (260,000 Christians, 900 churches, 150 church missions committees) and 19 missions agencies.

2. How effective is your cooperative effort among churches and missions agencies in your country? Do you have a national missions association to represent many missions agencies?

Hong Kong Association of Christian Missions is the major coordinating body of all missions agencies and 80 percent of the missions-minded churches in Hong Kong. The Association aims at hastening cooperation between various agencies in the areas of promotion, education, and training of missionary candidates. The response is satisfactory.

3. What can AMA and EFA Missions Commission do to help your national missionary movement and missions association?

They can help in the area of training missionary candidates.

4. How can your national missions associations cooperate with denominations and missionary associations from the West?

Information exchange, research, and forming of international teams for evangelism.

5. Do you see a need to promote cooperation among missions agencies in the Third World?

Definitely yes, especially in the areas of financing, training, supervision, care of missionaries, and information exchange and research.

2-8. Interview with Dr. Hong Shik Shin (long-time missionary to Thailand), May 3, 1991, Seoul, Korea

1. Can you describe the recent growth of the foreign missionary movement in Thailand with number of missionaries and missions agencies?

The concern for foreign missions in Thailand is quite weak. The participants to the last AMC have just begun to realize the need for missions. Only one Thai missionary has gone out although there are about 800 churches in Thailand.

2. What is the situation with the Korean missionaries in Thailand?

There are some 30 Korean missionary families. They were sent by about seven Korean denominations and two Korean missions societies. They have only fellowship through the Korean Missionary Fellowship in Thailand but do not cooperate in their ministries. They are supported and controlled by the Korean churches or societies. Field ministries are left in the hands of the missionaries.

3. What is the relationship between the Korean missionaries and the Thai churches?

About five Korean missionary families belong to the Church of Christ of Thailand (CCT) and partnership with them. One Korean family belongs to a native Thai Church and partnerships with it. The rest do not partnership with Thai churches but carry out their missions independently even though they are under the umbrella of the Evangelical Fellowship of Thailand for legal purposes. It is understandable that many of them work independently from CCT and are merely under an umbrella of the EFT, because the CCT is favorable to the World Council of Churches (WCC) and has a strong denominational policy. Quite a number of Korean missionaries from the same Korean denomination work independently without partnership among themselves.

4. What is your proposal for partnership in missions?

Ecumenical theology of mission stresses unity. As a result cooperation and partnership are well practiced while the doctrinal standpoint is weak. Evangelical theology of mission stresses evangelical faith. As a result cooperation and partnership are not well practiced and often duplications of ministry are made. Evangelical missionaries, therefore, should learn from traditional mission societies, analyze their strong and weak points, and try to develop and establish cooperation and partnership in missions.

5. What is your proposal to the Western missions leaders?

Western missions should not absorb Two-Thirds world missions forces or resources into international missions. They should rather encourage these national missions to develop into mature missions similar to the international missions. They should stress and practice equality, mutuality, and partnership in missions with the Two-Thirds world national missions.

OMF, for example, should not absorb the Korean missions resources into OMF but encourage the Korean Churches to build a national missions society similar to OMF. The Western missions society, for example, could loan missions specialists to the national missions society.

6. What is the relationship between denominations and missions societies?

Missions societies are not normal phenomena. If churches are awakened and alert doing missions, missions societies are not needed. Both bodies, however, should respect each other. The church should recognize the special function of missions and can commit missions tasks to them. Missions societies should also humbly respect churches and carry out committed tasks together. Agreement should be made between them on concrete terms.

Conclusions

Many Asians serve as missionaries. About 700 Korean families and about 400 Japanese families have gone out as cross-cultural missionaries. In one month (April, 1991) eight Koreans were sent out to the Soviet Union as missionaries to serve the Russian-speaking Koreans in six different cities.

As Asian missions leaders have expressed, however, cooperation and genuine partnership in missions is not yet practiced. Partnership among national churches, between churches and missions societies, and between national churches and Western missions societies is not yet well established. In many cases competition and conflicts are still manifested, and duplications of ministry result...

Leaders all admit the need of partnership in missions to do missions rightly because we live in an age of internationalization and because ministry is becoming more diversified and mutually related. In this age of religious and ideological plurality, a demonstration of Christian unity is crucial for evangelism.

APPENDIX C

Harnessing Filipino missionary potential
– a new movement picks up steam

Reprinted with permission from *Pulse* (Wheaton, IL: Evangelical Missions Information Service), August 24, 1990

Everywhere you go around the world, you find Filipinos, says Met Castillo, general secretary of the Philippine Missions Association and field chairman of Philippine Crusades. There is a natural desire to travel and discover other cultures. Now mission agencies are learning how to harness those typically Filipino skills and interests for the cause of world missions.

When did the modern Philippine missionary movement begin?

Missionaries were being sent as early as 1968, but the missions movement as a national impetus did not really start until the 1980s. The Philippine Missions Association was founded in 1983, and then local churches began to think about missions. At that time, we began to conduct missions awareness seminars for local churches and pastors.

What is the Philippine Missions Association?

PMA was founded as an umbrella organization of various small mission organizations in the Philippines. Its members are missions committees of local churches, denominational departments of missions, and independent missions boards. However, it is more than simply an association of missions. It is also a missionary sending agency. PMA is a unique organization; you won't find anything like it in the missiological books. Our main goal is to encourage our member groups to send missionaries and to assist them in sending their own missionaries. But, in cases where one or two member missions cannot do it on their own, we pool our resources and PMA becomes a sending organization. We also receive Asian missionaries. We have had Indonesian, Korean, and Singaporean missionaries working with us through separate working agreements.

How many Filipino missionaries are there currently and where do they work?

I would estimate there are about 700 missionaries, with about 500 working cross-culturally within the country. As to foreign missions, they are all over the world, with many in Southeast Asia. Latin America is opening up to us, especially because of natural bridges between the Filipino and Latin American cultures. Because of our Spanish background (the Philippines was a Spanish colony for 350 years), Filipinos have little difficulty learning the Spanish language. In fact, 12 to 16 units of Spanish is required for completion of a college degree in the Philippines. And centuries of Spanish rule have left a lot of Spanish culture in this country in terms of language, material life, social structures, and value systems. I encourage Filipino missionaries to go to Latin America. We are working cooperatively with some who are already there.

How do you handle the matter of finances?

We have three problems related to finances. First, we cannot legally send money out of the Philippines. Secondly, the Philippine economy is not good. And then, missions is still new here, and not many churches have made missions — or missions giving — a priority. We still have much work to do in this area. There are several ways of solving the first problem. One way is to enter into partnership, as for example, PMA and SIM International. When we send missionaries to their fields, we raise all the funds that will be spent within the Philippines, including air fare and the like. But the money needed to support the missionary on the field is raised outside the Philippines in cooperation with SIM International.

What is the advantage of working in partnership with a Western mission agency?

When I look at missions all over the world, I see a lot of missions money going to the support of missions structures — paying salaries of mission executives, renting offices of mission organizations, and the like. We believe our money should go to the support of missionaries rather than mission structures. In order to cut down on expenses and overhead, for example, when we send missionaries to Africa, we enter into a partnership agreement with a mission already working there. We simply provide the personnel to them, and they use them according to their program. That way, the little money we raise in Asia is used to support missionaries. Denominational groups in the Philippines use a similar framework, working cooperatively between the mission department of the national church and the founding Western mission or denominational mission board.

What sort of missionary training is offered in the Philippines?

The Asian Center for Missionary Education, which is a ministry of PMA, provides missions education for the entire church. One of its primary ministries is Missionary Training Modules, a series of 12 courses intended to provide practical training for missionary candidates. After completion of the courses and after appointment, the candidate does an internship.

What do you see as the future of the missions movement in the Philippines?

The missions movement here is growing rapidly. I believe one day it will be one of the major forces of missions in Asia, since we are gifted with personnel. When you think of missions resources in Asia, you can find countries that have greater financial resources, but not so many personnel. This is where the Philippines stands out. We have a project we began four years ago to send out 2,000 missionaries by the year 2000. We want to send 1,000 cross-culturally within the country and 1,000 outside the country. We call this the "2,000 by 2000 Plan."

APPENDIX D

PARTNER MISSION AGREEMENT
BETWEEN THE PHILIPPINES MISSION ASSOCIATION
(hereinafter referred to as PMA)
AND
SIM EAST ASIA LTD
(hereinafter referred to as SIM)

PREAMBLE:

The PMA and SIM seek to establish a Partner-Mission relationship to work together in the recruitment and support of cross-cultural missionaries to serve in the SIM areas of service in Africa, South America, and Asia, in order to achieve mutual goals in evangelism, church-planting, teaching, and supportive ministries to the Glory of God.

In accordance with this Partner Mission agreement, the PMA and SIM agree to administer cooperative ministries as follows:

MEMBER MISSIONARY RELATIONSHIP:

1. The missionary shall have dual membership status with both the PMA and SIM.

2. The appointment of the missionary shall be subject to the approval of both agencies in accordance with the standards established by each agency. A copy of the regulations of each agency will be supplied to the other.

3. In the event that the other agency requests confidential materials gathered by the other, such materials shall be shared with the understanding that the materials shall be kept confidential by that agency.

4. The missionary candidates shall participate in the full candidate and training program of both agencies.

5. Sufficient time shall be allowed for deputation work under the coordination of the PMA (in Philippines) and SIM (outside Philippines) in order that adequate prayer and financial support can be realized.

6. SIM shall supervise the securing of visas and make other arrangements necessary for the beginning of field work.

7. The PMA shall be the sending agency for financial and prayer support of the missionary.

8. SIM shall be the directing agency in relation to missionary activities and care in the area of service.

9. While on the field, and while travelling to and from the field, the missionary shall be under the jurisdiction of the SIM.

10. While on the field, the missionary shall be an integral part of the field staff sharing equally in privileges and responsibilities as any other member and being subject to the policies and direction of SIM.

11. The missionary's field director will initiate furlough planning in consultation with the PMA and SIM.

12. While on furlough, the missionary shall be under the jurisdiction of the PMA. Among the missionary's furlough responsibilities, consideration will be given by the PMA to assignments, projects, additional study, or training requested by the SIM. Progress reports and information during furlough will be provided to SIM.

13. While on furlough the missionary shall primarily carry on a deputation ministry for the PMA within the constituency of the PMA congregations. When requested by SIM to undertake additional deputation or activities, such expenses shall be SIM's responsibility.

14. The missionary shall not solicit for personal funds from homeland or constituencies of either agency without the permission of the respective agency.

15.1 The missionaries are to raise full support required from whatever sources available to them and by looking to God to supply all their needs.

15.2 Support raised in Philippines shall be kept for the following:
- outgoing   -administration
- furlough   -retirement benefits
- return air tickets   -deputation ministry

15.3 SIM will assist in raising financial support for PMA missionaries from churches and Christians in Asia and other countries. (See Appendix.) All PMA/SIM missionary appointees shall not leave for the field until their outgoing funds and 100% of their external financial support have been raised.

15.4 The field allowance for PMA missionaries will be the same as that for all other SIM members.

16. The PMA missionaries recommended for service with SIM would fully accept the SIM Manual, including the Doctrinal Statement, and agree to live and serve in accord with the policies and

practices contained therein. As an integrated Mission SIM does not have separate or denominational areas of work.

ADMINISTRATIVE MATTERS:

17. The SIM East Asia office in Singapore is responsible for all SIM's missionary sending relationships with countries in the Asia area.

18. The PMA will co-operate with SIM East Asia in the following:

a. Candidates:

- notify prospective candidates of service opportunities and giving full information.

- all inquirers will be dealt with directly through the Director for International Relations of the PMA.

- the Mission Board of PMA will screen, interview and appoint the candidates as PMA missionaries and then second them to work with SIM. In doing so, the PMA will accept the norms set up by SIM for confirmation of service opportunity from SIM East Asia.

- following acceptance by SIM, the PMA will be responsible for final preparation for service in the field in cooperation with SIM.

b. Missionaries:

- when in Philippines they will come under the direction of the PMA concerning furlough arrangements, additional training, deputation, etc.; but all matters relating to their status as SIM missionaries are to be discussed with SIM.

- when in the field will come under the direction of the SIM Area Director or International Liaison Officer (ILO): according to SIM's relationship with the National Church in the particular country.

- will receive SIM salary allowance monthly and copies of reports and prayer letters will be sent to the PMA, SIM Area National Offices.

- will receive furlough allowance according to PMA rate. Leftovers from salary portion of funds raised will be kept for deputation ministry, preparatory costs for return to field, and ministry funds.

19. The PMA will receive from SIM as needed:

- regular information concerning SIM programs

- copies of "SIM-NOW" magazine and other literatures as appropriate

- lists of vacancies in the field — approximately bi-monthly

- end of term reports on PMA missionaries

- open communication concerning all matters relating to PMA personnel

- annual assessment of total support requirement for each missionary for the following financial year (October 1 to September 30)

20. The PMA and SIM Area Offices:

a. All missionary assignments are made by the Area Council in the field or National Church and are communicated through the SIM East Asia office.

b. Length of term/furlough will be agreed with the Area Director. The length of term for PMA/SIM missionaries is normally four years with twelve months' furlough.

c. The missionary is responsible to the Area Director of ILO concerning all matters relating to his ministry and service in the field. The PMA will be informed well in advance before a missionary is transferred from one ministry to another except in an emergency.

d. PMA will issue receipts on behalf of SIM for Philippine donors and maintain proper records for SIM East Asia.

e. Any correspondence from the PMA to the SIM Area Office should be copied to the SIM East Asia office.

THE TENURE OF THIS AGREEMENT WOULD BE 5 (FIVE) YEARS AFTER WHICH IT WOULD BE REVIEWED AND RENEWED.

SIM East Asia   Philippines Missionary Association

DATE:

Appendix

To be updated in September of each year

A. The following financial needs are the administrative responsibility of SIM East Asia:
1. Salary allowance during field term
2. Field care costs, including medical and accommodation
3. Airfare home from field of service
4. East Asia office administrative costs
5. Ministry account needs during field term

B. The following financial needs are the administrative responsibility of PMA prior to departure:
1. Outgoing airfare and baggage costs
2. Essential clothing and equipment costs
3. Language study costs

The above costs will be calculated by PMA and SIM for each outgoing missionary.

C. The following financial needs are the administrative responsibility of the PMA during field service:

Regular support gifts from donors sufficient for:
1. PMA administrative costs
2. Funds to accumulate to pay salary allowance, accommodation and medical cost during furlough, plus a suitable retirement/insurance scheme.

D. The following financial needs are the administrative responsibility of PMA during furlough:
1. Airfare and baggage costs for return to the field
2. Equipment costs for return to field
3. Deputation cost

E. Although SIM helps in seeking for support, the missionaries are primarily responsible for maintaining their supporting constituency.

For More Information

Bosch, David J. *Transforming Mission: Paradigm Shifts in Theology of Mission.* Maryknoll, NY: Orbis Books, 1991.

Bush, Luis and Lorry Lutz. *Partnering in Ministry: the Direction of World Evangelism.* Downers Grove, IL: InterVarsity Press, 1990.

Bush, Luis. *Funding Third World Missions: the Pursuit of True Christian Partnership.* Singapore/Wheaton, IL: World Evangelical Fellowship Missions Commission, 1990.

Otis, George, Jr. *The Last of the Giants.* Tarrytown, NY: Chosen Books, 1991.

Pate, Larry. *From Every People: a Handbook of Two-Thirds World Missions.* Monrovia, CA: MARC, 1989.